THIS BOOK BEL

_____

MEDITATIONS
FOR THE PASSAGES
AND CELEBRATIONS
OF LIFE

Meditations for the Passages and Celebrations of Life

A BOOK OF VIGILS

NOELA N. EVANS

BELL TOWER · NEW YORK

Published by Bell Tower, an imprint of Harmony Books,
a division of Crown Publishers, Inc.,
201 East 50th Street, New York, New York 10022.
Member of the Crown Publishing Group.

Random House, Inc. New York, Toronto, London, Sydney, Auckland

Originally published in hardcover by Bell Tower in 1994

Bell Tower and colophon are trademarks of Crown Publishers, Inc.

Manufactured in the United States of America
Book and cover design by Debbie Glasserman

Library of Congress Cataloging-in-Publication Data
Evans, Noela N., 1944–
Meditations for the passages and celebrations of life : a book of vigils /
by Noela N. Evans. — 1st ed.
1. Meditations. I. Title.
BL624.2.E83 1994
291.4'3—dc20
93-4332
CIP

ISBN 0-517-88299-x
10 9 8 7 6 5 4 3 2 1
First Paperback Edition 1995

For
Jayne Clare Evans,
William Noel Evans,
and
Kiel Martin,
an unexpected friend

Contents

C O N T E N T S ....

Preface

IN THE LANGUAGE of astronomy there is a term used to describe the place where light is unable to escape the grasp of a black hole. It is called the "event horizon" and it is beautifully descriptive because this surface is actually a horizon beyond which we are unable to perceive any events.

In the galaxies of our hearts and minds we can sometimes feel as though we are balanced on a rim, unable either to escape or to see beyond the boundary. While we are blessed with wisdom from elders, counselors, family, and the worlds of print and media, each individual passage is distinct. There is no exact map or chart, no answer for the puzzle to be found at the back of the book. We ourselves are the puzzle, and, as every puzzle enthusiast knows, the solution requires attention, focus, and intuition.

I offer these vigils in the hope that they will lead you to the place in yourself where you are your *own* elder, counselor, and sage. Their observance provides a way to sit with each passage with attention, honesty, and tenderness, whether it be one of sorrow or joy. We find the time to share important moments with those we love and even those we don't love. Why not do so with ourselves?

Life in these times can be very fast. We rise with the day's agenda tumbling through our minds, eat on the run, and cling to our lists and appointment books to make sense of schedules that are relentless in their demands. We struggle to care for our children and our elders, to achieve in the workplace, and to be as attentive to friends and personal interests as time allows. Often I hear those around me cry, "I manage, some-how, to get it all done, but I'm missing my life!"

It is to this cry that these vigils respond. To reserve a few moments each day to be present with our personal events can provide a ribbon of continuity through the changes that alter the shape of our world and a center of stillness in the drama that seems to accompany these changes. This stillness may be deepened if you are able to sit quietly after the readings, observing your breath as it travels in and out, calmly watching and waiting in the spirit of "keeping vigil." If the language of a particular vigil is not entirely appropriate for your circum-stance, feel free to use it as a springboard to your own words.

The inspiration for this work comes from *The New American Book of the Dead*, which helped me to regain my balance after the death of my mother. A brief explanation of the similarities and differences between *The New American Book of the Dead* (IDHHB, Inc., 1981) and this book as well as information about the format of the readings may be found in the introduction to the chapter on death.

In writing the vigils I have made several important assumptions:

> That God really exists, although each of us may see the form and gender of this divinity a little differently.
> That the essence of who we are is eternal.
> That our lives count more than we can possibly imagine.
> That we all experience similar passages and celebrations and our responses to these events link us to each other in a way that nothing else can.

Several years ago my son began to study sleight of hand, and it wasn't long before his cards and coins were always in his pocket. I enjoyed watching the faces of those he dazzled with his wonders, and I enjoyed being dazzled myself. Most of all,

I enjoyed the vitality that seems as much a part of the performance as the magic itself. This vitality, I discovered, is the child of attention.

I cannot promise that your vigils will make the hard times disappear or that they will multiply the joyful ones, but I would remind you that your fully awakened presence is not only powerful, it can be magic.

Death

I REMEMBER HEARING somewhere that "the quality of your attention is the greatest compliment you can give." Lost in confusion and hurt after the death of my mother, I found that I needed to *do* something other than grieve, wrestle with my emotions, and sort through her estate. In looking for a way to honor and compliment her life, I began the readings from *The New American Book of the Dead.*

The focus of those readings is to guide the departed soul on its journey. Much of the language was beyond my understanding (and I'm sure it would have been beyond the understanding of my mother), but the daily observance of the readings gave me a centeredness and a ritual that was a true comfort to my heart, and I began to feel that my mother—wherever she might be—was deeply touched by the quality of my devotion.

While honoring the power and dignity of *The New American Book of the Dead,* I felt I wanted to enlarge the context by developing a series of readings of this nature. I have retained the use of a recurring "mantra" of words to guide the reader in and out of each vigil.

It is not vital that the readings begin on the day of death. Begin them whenever the moment seems right, and if their ending seems premature, you may add some of your own or start them all over again.

In *The New American Book of the Dead* it is suggested that the vigils be done at the same time, morning and evening, in the same place in a carefully described context. As I travel for a living, I did the best I could. I have funny memories of my readings in unorthodox places and at strange times. However, what mattered was that they were observed with presence.

I say to you, begin and end each day with the vigil for that day, wherever you are and accompanied by whatever has special meaning for you. A candle has significance for some, a flower for others. I took my mother's picture along, and that seemed to feel just right. Most important, bring your attention, in its deepest measure.

THE FIRST DAY

I may not understand—but I honor that you have been called to the side of the Great One.

You should know that your life mattered and that the world around you was changed because you passed this way
I need to let you know that I am grieving and that I am unresolved. Feel me close.

I drop all judgments of you and greet you as the child of God that you are, wishing you peace and guidance on your journey home.

THE SECOND DAY

I may not understand—but I honor that you have been called to the side of the Great One.

I am wrapped now in your memories and your essence.
I feel lost in tears of disbelief and I remain very fragile.

I drop all judgments of you and greet you as the child of God that you are, wishing you peace and guidance on your journey home.

THE THIRD DAY

I may not understand—but I honor that you have been called to the side of the Great One.

Your participation in my life was a treasure beyond words and I hope you can feel my appreciation.
Quite simply, I miss you and I ache for you.

I drop all judgments of you and greet you as the child of God that you are, wishing you peace and guidance on your journey home.

THE FOURTH DAY

I may not understand—but I honor that you have been called to the side of the Great One.

I see so many things that remind me of you. How very deeply you touched my heart.
I feel dazed and somehow less than whole. And often I hurt so much it frightens me.

I am told that just beyond these feelings there is a caring
presence that can comfort and calm me.
I will be as still as possible and seek that comfort and calm.

*I drop all judgments of you and greet you as the child of God that
you are, wishing you peace and guidance on your journey home.*

THE FIFTH DAY

*I may not understand—but I honor that you have been called to the
side of the Great One.*

My emotions are confusing and swing from sorrow to regret
to anger.
Letting them flow in honesty is healing for me and I know you
will understand that.

*I drop all judgments of you and greet you as the child of God that
you are, wishing you peace and guidance on your journey home.*

THE SIXTH DAY

*I may not understand—but I honor that you have been called to the
side of the Great One.*

My disbelief in the fact that you are gone mingles with the memories of your gestures, your smile, and the things that meant so much to you.
I am often uncertain about how I fit into life without you here.

I drop all judgments of you and greet you as the child of God that you are, wishing you peace and guidance on your journey home.

THE SEVENTH DAY

I may not understand—but I honor that you have been called to the side of the Great One.

I trust, with all that's in me to trust, that you can feel these vigils for you as an offering of my highest esteem.
A week has passed now since the beginning of my vigils and I am reminded that life moves in circles. May the circle of this first week be the beginning of my healing.

I drop all judgments of you and greet you as the child of God that you are, wishing you peace and guidance on your journey home.

THE EIGHTH DAY

I may not understand—but I honor that you have been called to the side of the Great One.

A week ago today I began my vigils for you who have slipped to an unknown that is beyond my grasp.
I acknowledge that my life continues here as I struggle to create a bridge by which to feel close to you.

I drop all judgments of you and greet you as the child of God that you are, wishing you peace and guidance on your journey home.

THE NINTH DAY

I may not understand—but I honor that you have been called to the side of the Great One.

Your life surrounded and enriched mine and those close to you in so many ways.
I think of the funny twists and turns in our times with each other. For a moment I am completely lost in thoughts of you. We are together.

I drop all judgments of you and greet you as the child of God that you are, wishing you peace and guidance on your journey home.

THE TENTH DAY

I may not understand—but I honor that you have been called to the side of the Great One.

I send greetings and blessings across our invisible bridge. The fact that you are no longer here often seems so unreal.

I drop all judgments of you and greet you as the child of God that you are, wishing you peace and guidance on your journey home.

THE ELEVENTH DAY

I may not understand—but I honor that you have been called to the side of the Great One.

I am so unsettled here. I wonder if the same is true for you. I surrender to that light I know holds us both, and ask that it bring rest, relief, and resolution.

I drop all judgments of you and greet you as the child of God that you are, wishing you peace and guidance on your journey home.

THE TWELFTH DAY

I may not understand—but I honor that you have been called to the side of the Great One.

I thank you for your many gifts, but most of all for the love
I felt in your eyes.
Now my eyes are filled with tears, sometimes at the most
surprising moments.
I have learned to accept and appreciate these tears just as I
accepted and appreciated your love.

*I drop all judgments of you and greet you as the child of God that
you are, wishing you peace and guidance on your journey home.*

THE THIRTEENTH DAY

*I may not understand—but I honor that you have been called to the
side of the Great One.*

Your memory becomes the dearest of jewels.
Others offer advice and comfort. Sometimes it makes sense
and sometimes not, but I understand their concern for me,
and that makes me feel a little less alone.

*I drop all judgments of you and greet you as the child of God that
you are, wishing you peace and guidance on your journey home*

THE FOURTEENTH DAY

I may not understand—but I honor that you have been called to the side of the Great One.

I come, once again, to honor you with my vigil.
The circle of the second week closes and I offer up my emptiness to the healing rhythms of the light that holds us both.

I drop all judgments of you and greet you as the child of God that you are, wishing you peace and guidance on your journey home.

THE FIFTEENTH DAY

I may not understand—but I honor that you have been called to the side of the Great One.

Perhaps there are things that are unresolved for you, uncompleted.
But it is my pleasure to remind you that you saw some of your dreams come true.
One of my dreams come true was having you in my life.

I drop all judgments of you and greet you as the child of God that you are, wishing you peace and guidance on your journey home.

THE SIXTEENTH DAY

I may not understand—but I honor that you have been called to the side of the Great One.

You will always have a home in my heart, and I visit you there when all is quiet.
Here, life goes on, but I remain one step removed.
Losing you has touched my soul and I need time to accept this change.

I drop all judgments of you and greet you as the child of God that you are, wishing you peace and guidance on your journey home.

THE SEVENTEENTH DAY

I may not understand—but I honor that you have been called to the side of the Great One.

I hope when the memories of your life here rise in your heart, you feel a smile, a fondness, and a pride that you were part of all this.
I am beginning to notice the world around me: The color has come back just a bit, and I am glad for that.

I drop all judgments of you and greet you as the child of God that you are, wishing you peace and guidance on your journey home.

THE EIGHTEENTH DAY

I may not understand—but I honor that you have been called to the side of the Great One.

I think of the things I learned from you and hope you know what value they have for me.
These teachings are alive and I think about them in ways I never did before.

I drop all judgments of you and greet you as the child of God that you are, wishing you peace and guidance on your journey home.

THE NINETEENTH DAY

I may not understand—but I honor that you have been called to the side of the Great One.

Sometimes I can bring the clear image of your face into my mind's eye, and sometimes I cannot.
But your essence is always within reach. I am beginning to

understand that our relationship has not ended—it has simply changed.

I drop all judgments of you and greet you as the child of God that you are, wishing you peace and guidance on your journey home.

THE TWENTIETH DAY

I may not understand—but I honor that you have been called to the side of the Great One.

I wonder if you know that I forgive you for all misdeeds, real and imagined.
I hope and trust that this forgiveness also extends from you to me.

I drop all judgments of you and greet you as the child of God that you are, wishing you peace and guidance on your journey home.

THE TWENTY-FIRST DAY

I may not understand—but I honor that you have been called to the side of the Great One.

The third circle closes in these vigils, my gift to you—and to myself.

DEATH ···

I trust my feelings and my habits a little more now and I have new appreciation for the small details of life that are beginning to lead me back into the world.

I drop all judgments of you and greet you as the child of God that you are, wishing you peace and guidance on your journey home.

THE TWENTY-SECOND DAY

I may not understand—but I honor that you have been called to the side of the Great One.

I hope that you are well and that you can feel my concern. Your well-being was important to me in your life and it is no less so in your death.
I am just beginning to ask for the courage to accept this change.

I drop all judgments of you and greet you as the child of God that you are, wishing you peace and guidance on your journey home.

THE TWENTY-THIRD DAY

I may not understand—but I honor that you have been called to the side of the Great One.

I know that you have taken your understanding and strength with you, and that you are rich, wherever you are. You have everything you need for whatever unfolds for you now.
Though still unsettled, I acknowledge my own strength and trust it to provide the support I need at this time.

I drop all judgments of you and greet you as the child of God that you are, wishing you peace and guidance on your journey home.

THE TWENTY-FOURTH DAY

I may not understand—but I honor that you have been called to the side of the Great One.

The things you cared about have such meaning in my life. Sometimes I find myself having animated dialogues with you in my head.
And so we go on, you and I, from different perspectives, but linked by our history and our love.

I drop all judgments of you and greet you as the child of God that you are, wishing you peace and guidance on your journey home.

THE TWENTY-FIFTH DAY

I may not understand—but I honor that you have been called to the side of the Great One.

I can laugh sometimes now, and mean it.
I am beginning to understand the blessing of the passing of time; not that it makes me forget, but that it lends perspective and shows how to integrate your memories into my world.

I drop all judgments of you and greet you as the child of God that you are, wishing you peace and guidance on your journey home.

THE TWENTY-SIXTH DAY

I may not understand—but I honor that you have been called to the side of the Great One.

It is time now for me to share with you, in my own words, what is deepest in my heart:

....

I drop all judgments of you and greet you as the child of God that you are, wishing you peace and guidance on your journey home.

THE TWENTY-SEVENTH DAY

I may not understand—but I honor that you have been called to the side of the Great One.

The love and respect I feel for you can only deepen.
I acknowledge that even though my vigils are coming to a close, the process of this transition will take—as long as it takes.
I promise myself patience and understanding and hopefulness.

I drop all judgments of you and greet you as the child of God that you are, wishing you peace and guidance on your journey home.

THE TWENTY-EIGHTH DAY

I may not understand—but I honor that you have been called to the side of the Great One.

"The heart remembers, one who is loved never dies."[1]
I bless you, I release you, I carry you always and forever in all that is dearest to me.

I drop all judgments of you and greet you as the child of God that you are, wishing you peace and guidance on your journey home.

Birth

BIRTH IS CERTAINLY a time when it is easy to get lost in the amazing change that has come into your life. I invite you to step for a moment, morning and evening, into the vigils of welcoming.

Thousands of babies make their way into thousands of lives every day, yet each child is like a snowflake, a marvel all its own. My son was born in October, and when my birthday arrived in December, my mother sent me the following message: "Only now can you know how I felt on this day twenty-six years ago." Suddenly my childhood and the way I related to my mother were completely different. The feelings I had for my own child connected me to the feelings my mother had for me, before they became confused and tangled in years of mother-daughter dramas.

It is my hope that through these vigils you can more fully experience and claim the wonder of your child coming into the world and that you will pause to embrace the feelings and awakenings that surround this event. The vigils are written in the first person singular, so that no matter what your relation to the newborn, they are appropriate. The individual circumstances of giving birth vary widely. These readings are structured to begin the day following the birth as this may be a quieter and more receptive time to initiate them than the birth day itself.

Being present in the vigils is a statement to yourself and your child that you will be present in your life together, that the quality of your attention will be something you can both count on. What greater gift can you give than this?

THE FIRST DAY

I celebrate and welcome the new life that has come into mine!

Together we share in our private miracle. I am filled with wonder and amazement. After all this time of waiting, you are here. Hello, dear child.

I love you. I believe in you. I wish only the best for you.

THE SECOND DAY

I celebrate and welcome the new life that has come into mine!

When I gaze into your eyes, you seem as old as you are young. I acknowledge that you have as much to teach and show me as I have to teach and show you.
I promise to honor this truth. It is my first pledge to you.

I love you. I believe in you. I wish only the best for you.

THE THIRD DAY

I celebrate and welcome the new life that has come into mine!

The responsibility for your care is one I take up with great joy and hope, and I ask for lifelong guidance from the Great Parent, the Source of all life.

I love you. I believe in you. I wish only the best for you.

THE FOURTH DAY

I celebrate and welcome the new life that has come into mine!

How strange and new this all feels—and, at the same time, how familiar. I will embrace the familiarity and trust it to help me make the many decisions and choices that are required as you are woven into my day-to-day life.

I love you. I believe in you. I wish only the best for you.

THE FIFTH DAY

I celebrate and welcome the new life that has come into mine!

Let us bond with each other in all the ways we need, and I will somehow find the quiet moments for these bonds to form. I invite your trust and your love.

I love you. I believe in you. I wish only the best for you.

THE SIXTH DAY

I celebrate and welcome the new life that has come into mine!

I acknowledge that I have to make the transition from childbirth to child caring with its many demands and responsibilities.
I will not feel guilt in providing for my own needs. I know that my being well-balanced means the best of all parenting for you.

I love you. I believe in you. I wish only the best for you.

THE SEVENTH DAY

I celebrate and welcome the new life that has come into mine!

Happy birthday! How amazing to know someone right from the moment of birth.

I am your oldest friend. I think of the birthdays that stretch ahead and somehow know that the time will all pass so fast. I promise to savor it as much as I can—putting you and us first amid the busyness of my days.

I love you. I believe in you. I wish only the best for you.

THE EIGHTH DAY

I celebrate and welcome the new life that has come into mine!

It is with such pride that I present you to our family and friends.
I know their participation in your life will be a richness.
I will allow them their own relationship with you and hope that their perspective will enlarge my own.

I love you. I believe in you. I wish only the best for you.

THE NINTH DAY

I celebrate and welcome the new life that has come into mine!

I reach back into my own childhood to retrieve the best of my upbringing and to pardon and discard the parts I've always felt were not in harmony with what I needed.

I know that I will be influenced by the way I was cared for and I trust my memories to guide and teach me.

I love you. I believe in you. I wish only the best for you.

THE TENTH DAY

I celebrate and welcome the new life that has come into mine!

You become more familiar to me each day and I am beginning to experience fully what it is to love my child.
It is a love unlike any other and I am deeply grateful to have the chance to know it.

I love you. I believe in you. I wish only the best for you.

THE ELEVENTH DAY

I celebrate and welcome the new life that has come into mine!

You seem to come more alive each day now, and there is so much I want to show you and share with you.
I ask for blessings on this long journey of mutual discovery.

I love you. I believe in you. I wish only the best for you.

THE TWELFTH DAY

I celebrate and welcome the new life that has come into mine!

Though you do not yet communicate in words, I feel that I usually understand your needs.
The times when I do not understand are frustrating for me and probably also for you, and I need to acknowledge that.
I will do the best I can, knowing I will be guided through the frustration and the anger.

I love you. I believe in you. I wish only the best for you.

THE THIRTEENTH DAY

I celebrate and welcome the new life that has come into mine!

I can still be surprised by this wonderful change that has come into my world and the accompanying shift in my emotional weather. And the tiredness I feel. And the awe.
I ask for help in recognizing that this is all part of the process.

I love you. I believe in you. I wish only the best for you.

THE FOURTEENTH DAY

I celebrate and welcome the new life that has come into mine!

Another birthday for you—another week for us of settling into being a family.
May you feel your place in that and know that it is a place all your own.

I love you. I believe in you. I wish only the best for you.

THE FIFTEENTH DAY

I celebrate and welcome the new life that has come into mine!

Although you are the center of my world right now, I realize that descriptions of your every move are not necessarily appropriate in all conversations.
I ask for balance in this matter and for the chance to acknowledge that others in my life have their own news that is precious and meaningful to them.

I love you. I believe in you. I wish only the best for you.

THE SIXTEENTH DAY

I celebrate and welcome the new life that has come into mine!

I see you change day by day and I delight in your accomplishments.
I understand that you have your own inner schedule.
While encouraging you, I promise to try not to pressure you or compare you with others who have different timetables.

I love you. I believe in you. I wish only the best for you.

THE SEVENTEENTH DAY

I celebrate and welcome the new life that has come into mine!

What a link to wonder you are and what a treasure that is.
You are a living, breathing beginning! Like spring, like dawn.
We have so many "firsts" to embrace together and I will try to savor each one with the excitement and attention it deserves.

I love you. I believe in you. I wish only the best for you.

THE EIGHTEENTH DAY

I celebrate and welcome the new life that has come into mine!

Advice, suggestions, and words of wisdom: Friends and family can seem full of these. I appreciate that they are offering the gifts of their experience and intuition.
While honoring that their counsel has value and may expand my field of knowing, I trust myself to know how to be with you.

I love you. I believe in you. I wish only the best for you.

THE NINETEENTH DAY

I celebrate and welcome the new life that has come into mine!

Sometimes my concern for your well-being overwhelms me. I want everything to be perfect for you.
But perfection exists only in the essence of the Great One, so I practice turning over your ultimate care to that essence, which guides, protects, and ennobles us all.

I love you. I believe in you. I wish only the best for you.

THE TWENTIETH DAY

I celebrate and welcome the new life that has come into mine!

I cannot know what skills you will need to thrive in a world
that may be very different when you grow up.
I do know you will be faced with an ever-expanding array of
choices, and I will try to teach you how to make choices
wisely, how to take responsibility for your decisions, and how
to learn from your mistakes.

I love you. I believe in you. I wish only the best for you.

THE TWENTY-FIRST DAY

I celebrate and welcome the new life that has come into mine!

How long I waited to know you, and now we celebrate three
weeks of birthdays together.
Celebrate. What a wonderful word!
What joy it will be to introduce you to the holidays and
festivals that are central to my life, and to share with you what
"celebrate" means for me.

I love you. I believe in you. I wish only the best for you.

THE TWENTY-SECOND DAY

I celebrate and welcome the new life that has come into mine!

The world around me calls. I am supposed to be getting back to "normal." I understand this, but I reserve the right to remember vividly this dazzling experience of birth. It is my private epic motion picture that I can run on the screen of my mind whenever my heart needs a lift.

I love you. I believe in you. I wish only the best for you.

THE TWENTY-THIRD DAY

I celebrate and welcome the new life that has come into mine!

One of the lessons you will need to learn is about sharing—and I need to learn this lesson, too.
There are those around us who are entitled to be involved as you grow and change, and I need to feel secure enough to share you with them.
My role in your world is distinct and irreplaceable, and re-membering that can make my sharing easier.

I love you. I believe in you. I wish only the best for you.

THE TWENTY-FOURTH DAY

I celebrate and welcome the new life that has come into mine!

It will be some time before you can express yourself in words, but I think ahead to the times when you will and I look forward to talking with you—not just as child and parent, but as two people sharing what is in our hearts.

I know to be friends with someone you are related to is not always easy, but I will do what I can to help our friendship unfold.

I love you. I believe in you. I wish only the best for you.

THE TWENTY-FIFTH DAY

I celebrate and welcome the new life that has come into mine!

I want to take a moment to think about laughter and discovery and magic, and hugging and play and downright silliness.
And to tell you that I know how important and necessary these are.

If I am really lucky, maybe you will take me with you sometimes when you begin to wander into your own world, where these things count so much.

I love you. I believe in you. I wish only the best for you.

THE TWENTY-SIXTH DAY

I celebrate and welcome the new life that has come into mine!

As my vigils draw to a close, it is time to say to you in my own words what is deepest in my heart:

....

I love you. I believe in you. I wish only the best for you.

THE TWENTY-SEVENTH DAY

I celebrate and welcome the new life that has come into mine!

I know that I must set limits for you until you are able to set them for yourself. I recognize your need for discipline and I will strive to be fair and consistent.
Take my hand as we begin our journey together. I will try to live what I have to teach you, knowing that you may not always hear what I say, but you will be watching every move I make!

I love you. I believe in you. I wish only the best for you.

THE TWENTY-EIGHTH DAY

I celebrate and welcome the new life that has come into mine!

You may look like me or have gestures that are similar, but you are uniquely you.
I cannot live your life and I will not try.
My guidance, my love, and your freedom is the threefold pledge I make on this, the last of my vigils to welcome you into the world.

I love you. I believe in you. I wish only the best for you.

Marriage

HOW STARTLING IT is to discover that just because we have found the love of our dreams, we are not guaranteed a happily-ever-after. We hear this caution whispered, but we hope that somehow we will be the exception.

Naturally, marriage involves sharing, loving, and self-sacrifice. It asks that we care for and nurture a partner through heaven only knows what kinds of hills and valleys. Moreover, what society is just beginning to understand is that a committed relationship is perhaps the most action-packed road to our own self-discovery.

As I wrote this chapter I spoke with many couples about their lives together and I began to understand that the more fully you risk revealing yourself through all your changes, uncertainties, and conquests, and the better you are able to provide a climate for your partner to do the same, the more adventurous your marriage will be. An alive marriage is a study in day-to-day risk, and risk enlarges the soul.

These vigils are structured to begin four weeks before the wedding. If it is to be a ring ceremony, you may wish to hold the ring you will give gently in your hand, or light a candle as a symbol of the light you carry in your heart for each other. Whatever small touches you add to the setting for your vigils, add them with care and tenderness.

The week before I climbed a mountain overlooking the Pacific to take my vows as a young bride, a favorite elder told me a story about a pot, a pot that stands between two people who share their lives. In the beginning it is full of the excitement and joy of the wedding and their new life together, but the stresses and demands of living sometimes leave the couple little time to think about the pot, and one day they discover it is empty.

Sure enough, the response is disappointment and anger. "Why doesn't *she* do something?" he wonders. "How could *he* have let this happen?" she moans. And the secret here is to give up waiting for the *other* person to respond. No matter how tired or distracted you feel, toss a little something in the pot—a kindness, an embrace, the lovingly phrased determination to work out a point of difference, because it's a magic pot, of course, and small contributions attract others of their kind, which then multiply, and in this way the "pot" of the relationship remains full, interesting, and nourishing.

To be mindful of the "pot" calls for awareness in the midst of the details of life that take so much time and thought. To be mindful of the "pot" calls for us to remember our marriage promises with loving attention.

Elizabeth Cogburn, founder of the Tree of Life Ceremonials, has said that "love without awareness is suffering." As you pledge your hearts to each other, pledge also your awareness and the commitment to expand its depth and quality through all the years of your lives.

THE TWENTY-EIGHTH DAY

I bring my heart and I bring my freedom to walk with you through time.

This is a journey of the soul into the mysteries of union, and, like all journeys into the unknown, it will have its dangers and its delights.
Our compassion and our individual freedom are essential to its success.

I honor your heart and your freedom with my love and my faith in our life together.

THE TWENTY-SEVENTH DAY

I bring my heart and I bring my freedom to walk with you through time.

At the beginning of the vigils for our marriage it feels appropriate to remember the parents, elders, and siblings (those of blood and those of heart) and the circumstances that have shaped me, and all those who have, in turn, shaped you.
I am grateful that the pathways of our lives have led us to each other.

I honor your heart and your freedom with my love and my faith in our life together.

THE TWENTY-SIXTH DAY

I bring my heart and I bring my freedom to walk with you through time.

These vigils are a way of acknowledging that I have sat with the decision to marry you in the deepest and quietest parts of who I am.
I ask for the maturity this commitment calls forth and I invite its challenge and nourishment.

I honor your heart and your freedom with my love and my faith in our life together.

THE TWENTY-FIFTH DAY

I bring my heart and I bring my freedom to walk with you through time.

Our wedding is not really about two becoming one, but about two becoming three. There is me, there is you, and there is our marriage with a life and character of its own.
I pledge to nurture and be responsive to the needs of this very tender "third," to make choices that protect it, and to create a climate where it can unfold in beauty and safety under the guidance of the Eternal One.

I honor your heart and your freedom with my love and my faith in our life together.

THE TWENTY-FOURTH DAY

I bring my heart and I bring my freedom to walk with you through time.

I will no longer live as a closed system with friends, parents, and counselors at arm's length.
My life will now unfold in the daily witness of another. I ask

for the daring to accept this intimacy and embrace it as a gateway to revelation and discovery.

I honor your heart and your freedom with my love and my faith in our life together.

THE TWENTY-THIRD DAY

I bring my heart and I bring my freedom to walk with you through time.

Our love is encircled now with confidence, but I know there may be times of distance between us and confusion.
I hope we can create a place where we will find each other again when we are lost—in the mountains, in our church or temple, along the shore, beside our favorite tree, in a private joke we share, or in a song that calls us back.

I honor your heart and your freedom with my love and my faith in our life together.

THE TWENTY-SECOND DAY

I bring my heart and I bring my freedom to walk with you through time.

Forever and never-ending and everlasting: These words evoke feelings of comfort and of uncertainty. How can I pledge to concepts that lie outside the boundaries of tangible understanding?

There is reassurance in remembering that today and yesterday and tomorrow are all places on the way to forever.

Being alive to the possibilities, the risks, and the rewards of life each day creates a bridge where I can cross safely to the unknown in myself and our relationship.

I honor your heart and your freedom with my love and my faith in our life together.

THE TWENTY-FIRST DAY

I bring my heart and I bring my freedom to walk with you through time.

"It all begins at home." My response to the world starts with us —the way we talk to each other, the way we forgive, the way we hope and plan.

As I become increasingly skillful at relating to you and to the others who may come to share our home, I take a step forward as a citizen of my country and my world.

I honor your heart and your freedom with my love and my faith in our life together.

THE TWENTIETH DAY

I bring my heart and I bring my freedom to walk with you through time.

And I bring my humor, too! Laughter is the heart at play.
To laugh together is to seal our friendship with our own style of wit and playfulness.
Humor can enliven the good days and pull us through the rough ones.
When I look back on the sounds of our marriage, may laughter echo through my memories.

I honor your heart and your freedom with my love and my faith in our life together.

THE NINETEENTH DAY

I bring my heart and I bring my freedom to walk with you through time.

We have interests and passions in common, and then we have those that call us separately.

I cannot expect you to share all my enthusiasms, but I hope you will respect them, and I will try to extend my respect to yours.

I honor your heart and your freedom with my love and my faith in our life together.

THE EIGHTEENTH DAY

I bring my heart and I bring my freedom to walk with you through time.

Limits are part of living and my response to them can determine if mine is to be a life of disappointment and blame or one of challenge and reward.

It is said that to a great extent we choose the quality of our lives.

May I respond to the limits in my relationship with determination, poise, and an open mind.

May I choose limits that free.

May I invite limits that call me to the place where challenge and nourishment are one.

I honor your heart and your freedom with my love and my faith in our life together.

THE SEVENTEENTH DAY

I bring my heart and I bring my freedom to walk with you through time.

To forgive is to touch the vital spirit of God.
To truly let go of my hurts, real and imagined, requires that I acknowledge my own capacity to wound.
May we learn from our hurts and bless each other with our willingness to forgive.

I honor your heart and your freedom with my love and my faith in our life together.

THE SIXTEENTH DAY

I bring my heart and I bring my freedom to walk with you through time.

Sooner or later, money will probably be an issue. It is, after all, the dominant medium of exchange in the world, but it is not who we are.

Sound decisions about the practical things around us are part of a healthy relationship.
A sense of balance about the importance of money and what it will and won't provide is a part of that health.

I honor your heart and your freedom with my love and my faith in our life together.

THE FIFTEENTH DAY

I bring my heart and I bring my freedom to walk with you through time.

The invitation to share life with a separate and equal "other" is an adventure of the highest calling.
I may come to know every feature of your face, your nuances, idiosyncrasies, and patterns of the way you live day to day.
But I cannot truly know what it is like to be you.
And thank goodness! The quality of this unknown is an elixir that keeps our dance alive.

I honor your heart and your freedom with my love and my faith in our life together.

THE FOURTEENTH DAY

I bring my heart and I bring my freedom to walk with you through time.

Traditions add flavor like spices to soup. We bring many traditions from our families and backgrounds and embracing them is like a visit with an old and trusted friend.
But let me remember that together we can make up new traditions and when we do so, we enrich our lives with the magic of creating.
I am my own living history and my ceremonies and celebrations provide the moments to integrate experiences and discoveries into my life and to savor the richness and poignancy of the journey.

I honor your heart and your freedom with my love and my faith in our life together.

THE THIRTEENTH DAY

I bring my heart and I bring my freedom to walk with you through time.

To admit that I do not have all the answers is to awaken a freshness and an innocence that can lead to an elusive solution.

We each have our areas of expertise, but to be an expert about everything is to deny the power of the honesty that says, "I don't know."

May we bless our problems with this power and with the willingness to learn from a field of open inquiry.

I honor your heart and your freedom with my love and my faith in our life together.

THE TWELFTH DAY

I bring my heart and I bring my freedom to walk with you through time.

In the union of our bodies we explore the expression of our intimacy.

Tenderness and adventure and pleasure and release—and union.

It is here we behold the god and goddess in each other and touch the universal rhythm and cadence of life and creation.

I promise to make time and place for this private occasion of mystery and passion and to savor the delight of our bodies and souls coming together as one.

I honor your heart and your freedom with my love and my faith in our life together.

THE ELEVENTH DAY

I bring my heart and I bring my freedom to walk with you through time.

"Communication is the maintenance of love."[2] It is the art and skill of expression.
Do you always hear what I mean to say? How can we say things clearly to each other?
I will need to find the best times to share my news, my views, my questions, and my revelations.
We do not have the right to tell each other what to say, but gentle suggestions can be made about how and when to speak so that our message can be received without the distortions that can so often evoke confusion and defensiveness.

I honor your heart and your freedom with my love and my faith in our life together.

THE TENTH DAY

I bring my heart and I bring my freedom to walk with you through time.

Our occasional travels may take us far from each other, and I need to remember what renewal there can be in separation, to bless the time apart, and to rejoice in the opportunity to come together again.
Separations provide the time to reflect and to feel our love in a most vital way as I miss my partner, lover, and friend.

I honor your heart and your freedom with my love and my faith in our life together.

THE NINTH DAY

I bring my heart and I bring my freedom to walk with you through time.

To argue is to touch the face of our humanness in all its fury. A relationship begins to die when people stop talking about what bothers them. I am hopeful that we can disagree with openness and respect for the other's point of view.
But when this ideal fails, may I argue with valor, stick to the

subject at hand, and refrain as best I can from wounding you. Anger can provoke an honesty that is sometimes overdue. It can provide momentum to work through a discontent we have been ignoring.

And may I remember that it doesn't matter that we raised our voices, what matters is that our truth and fury can open a channel to resolution.

I honor your heart and your freedom with my love and my faith in our life together.

THE EIGHTH DAY

I bring my heart and I bring my freedom to walk with you through time.

I come to this sacred partnership with strength and resources, and also with hurts and unresolved dramas from yesterday and years ago.

Our life is a work in progress, and we each have our individual homework. I will not expect you to heal my wounded histories and I will respect your need to tend your own private garden.

We cannot do each other's inner work, though we can provide witness, understanding, and encouragement.

I honor your heart and your freedom with my love and my faith in our life together.

THE SEVENTH DAY

I bring my heart and I bring my freedom to walk with you through time.

It is one thing to commit. It is quite another to recommit. To recommit is to remember the promise I made to myself about my heart's desires; to pause amid the frustration, the stalemate, the distance that can grow between two people with the demands and stresses of life; to say yes to each other again, and to bless our marriage with love renewed.

I honor your heart and your freedom with my love and my faith in our life together.

THE SIXTH DAY

I bring my heart and I bring my freedom to walk with you through time.

I will need to discover what you do when you get scared.
We often feel that only children are entitled to be scared. We have no language for it in our adult world and hide in anger, depression, and anxiety.
This can be confusing to ourselves and to each other.
Being frightened calls for a different quality of support. I will try to be honest when I am scared and I invite you to do the same with me.

I honor your heart and your freedom with my love and my faith in our life together.

THE FIFTH DAY

I bring my heart and I bring my freedom to walk with you through time.

Courtesy is more than just good manners. It conveys a feeling of gracious respect.
We smile at people we don't know and usually respond politely to questions from strangers, but we can forget the value of diplomacy at home.

I will try to show the respect I feel for you, even when we are tired and out of sorts, because this is when courtesy is needed most.

I honor your heart and your freedom with my love and my faith in our life together.

THE FOURTH DAY

I bring my heart and I bring my freedom to walk with you through time.

My desires give birth to my vision. They provide valuable clues about who I am at a particular time.
To understand *why* I want what I want is to attend to their quality.
As we learn in our marriage to discriminate between the desires provoked by reaction and those that spring from the true spirit of who we are, we come to embrace those that reflect us at our best.

I honor your heart and your freedom with my love and my faith in our life together.

THE THIRD DAY

I bring my heart and I bring my freedom to walk with you through time.

In the history of humankind, we are part of a new and noble experiment.
Marriage has only recently developed from an obligation enforced by economics, family, and community to a partnership of love, trust, and shared hopes.
I will remember that all new creation requires patience, commitment, and the willingness to be baffled from time to time.

I honor your heart and your freedom with my love and my faith in our life together.

THE SECOND DAY

I bring my heart and I bring my freedom to walk with you through time.

This is the moment now for me to say, in my own words, what is deepest in my heart:

....

I honor your heart and your freedom with my love and my faith in our life together.

THE DAY BEFORE THE VOWS

I bring my heart and I bring my freedom to walk with you through time.

It is said that if you want to find the miraculous, look to the ordinary, but look with great attention.[3]
Hidden in the way we make up our lives together day by day are the strengths and the wonders of our union.
I promise to notice the small miracles and to cherish the satisfaction of the rhythm of our days, nights, seasons, and years.

I honor your heart and your freedom with my love and my faith in our life together.

THE DAY OF THE VOWS

I bring my heart and I bring my freedom to walk with you through time.

May the light of the One Spirit shine on the pathways to our
dreams.

May we rejoice in the opportunity and fullness of shared
expression.

May our strengths bless us with reward and wisdom.

May we rest in the grace of the One who holds and guides us.

May we know the sweetness and the power of a promise kept
for a lifetime.

*I honor your heart and your freedom with my love and my faith in
our life together.*

Moving

OUR HOMES ARE the stage for the most personal part of our lives. They are our nest. They can be a safe harbor or a battle zone, depending on the nature of the drama we are living at the time.

Leaving one home and moving to another stirs up a gamut of emotional response, which is why moving is so near the top of the "stress list." T.S. Eliot says, "In my end is my beginning," and I have a hunch that he is right. If we can do some focusing amid the chaos that usually accompanies a move, perhaps our transition will be a smoother one.

These vigils include a week of readings for the days before moving day and three weeks of readings for the new setting. Choose your own places for the readings, going from room to room. Perhaps you have already found the heart of your new home and want to deepen and confirm this with your vigils.

A move under bright circumstances or dreary ones is still a new beginning. Take a moment morning and evening to fill this beginning with your presence and attention. Think of it as a housewarming present to yourself.

SEVEN DAYS BEFORE THE DAY OF MOVING

The stage of my life is about to change; old doors are closing and new ones now stand open.

It is time to say good-bye to the best and the worst that happened to me in my old surroundings.
May this week be a time when the memories of this home flow through me, allowing me to feel them, to claim them, and to learn from them.

I honor this place that has sheltered me, and I embrace the changes and opportunities that this move invites into my life.

SIX DAYS BEFORE THE DAY OF MOVING

The stage of my life is about to change; old doors are closing and new ones now stand open.

As I go about my packing, I ask for the sword of discrimination to direct my choices.

May I strip away the things and ways of being that have grown stale and know with clarity the things and ways of being that will be welcomed and needed in my new environment.

I honor this place that has sheltered me, and I embrace the changes and opportunities that this move invites into my life.

FIVE DAYS BEFORE THE DAY OF MOVING

The stage of my life is about to change; old doors are closing and new ones now stand open.

This last week can seem chaotic. The organization I hoped for gets lost as I try to prepare for this move while juggling the parts of life and work that must go on as if nothing is changing.

May I use this moment of quiet to refocus and redirect.

I honor this place that has sheltered me, and I embrace the changes and opportunities that this move invites into my life.

FOUR DAYS BEFORE THE DAY OF MOVING

The stage of my life is about to change; old doors are closing and new ones now stand open.

I worry that there are things I need to take care of that will be overlooked and lost in all the activity.
I open myself to the guidance that will direct me, in balance, to care for the details that accompany this change.

I honor this place that has sheltered me, and I embrace the changes and opportunities that this move invites into my life.

THREE DAYS BEFORE THE DAY OF MOVING

The stage of my life is about to change; old doors are closing and new ones now stand open.

Today I reflect on the ways I changed during my stay in this place, the circumstances that brought me here, and now the events that have paved the way for this move.
I remember the person I was when I first walked through this door and acknowledge the person I have become.

I honor this place that has sheltered me, and I embrace the changes and opportunities that this move invites into my life.

TWO DAYS BEFORE THE DAY OF MOVING

The stage of my life is about to change; old doors are closing and new ones now stand open.

I walk from room to room gathering what is mine, allowing the space to return to a state of emptiness. I will try to leave it in a way that will be a good welcome for the next person who will call this home.

I honor this place that has sheltered me, and I embrace the changes and opportunities that this move invites into my life.

THE DAY BEFORE THE DAY OF MOVING

The stage of my life is about to change; old doors are closing and new ones now stand open.

I give thanks, one last time, for this dwelling place. I watch with tenderness as the setting for my days and nights turns into memory.
Good-bye, farewell, and may the life that follows me here be blessed.

I honor this place that has sheltered me, and I embrace the changes and opportunities that this move invites into my life.

THE DAY OF MOVING—THE FIRST DAY IN THE NEW HOME

The stage of my life has changed; old doors are closed and new ones now stand open.

Though I may have seen this space before, I now come to make it mine, to call it home.
Hello and greetings to the heart and soul of this new setting.

I honor this place that will shelter me, and I embrace the changes and opportunities that this move invites into my life.

THE SECOND DAY

The stage of my life has changed; old doors are closed and new ones now stand open.

Places are witnesses. They have silent stories to tell.
They absorb the events they have seen and reflect the personalities they have housed.
I invite a cleansing presence to come with me now throughout this home and I ask for the release of all stale energies and lingering darkness.

I honor this place that will shelter me, and I embrace the changes and opportunities that this move invites into my life.

THE THIRD DAY

The stage of my life has changed; old doors are closed and new ones now stand open.

I honor the past, the pathway that has brought me to this move, and greet this new place of being with hopeful expectation.

I honor this place that will shelter me, and I embrace the changes and opportunities that this move invites into my life.

THE FOURTH DAY

The stage of my life has changed; old doors are closed and new ones now stand open.

I consciously ask the Divine, with all its grace and protection, to move in with me along with my boxes and belongings.

I honor this place that will shelter me, and I embrace the changes and opportunities that this move invites into my life.

THE FIFTH DAY

The stage of my life has changed; old doors are closed and new ones now stand open.

I dedicate the vigil for today to the very best and brightest part of who I am. The reading of my vigils mirrors my desire for increased presence and awareness in this new setting.

I honor this place that will shelter me, and I embrace the changes and opportunities that this move invites into my life.

THE SIXTH DAY

The stage of my life has changed; old doors are closed and new ones now stand open.

There is so much to do and I am anxious to settle in. I will pause now to embrace this process.
And I will remember how much fun it can be to find new homes for all my old treasures, promising myself patience along the way.

I honor this place that will shelter me, and I embrace the changes and opportunities that this move invites into my life.

THE SEVENTH DAY

The stage of my life has changed; old doors are closed and new ones now stand open.

This completes the first week in my new home.
I will celebrate by reflecting on the sacredness of new beginnings and offering thanks.
Whether the circumstances that brought me here were born of pain or joy, it is, indeed, a new beginning, and I ask for blessings upon the person I will become under this roof.

I honor this place that will shelter me, and I embrace the changes and opportunities that this move invites into my life.

THE EIGHTH DAY

The stage of my life has changed; old doors are closed and new ones now stand open.

As I tried to leave behind outdated ways of being, I now consider habits I would like to change, virtues I would like to embrace, and joys I would like to see come to pass here.

I honor this place that will shelter me, and I embrace the changes and opportunities that this move invites into my life.

THE NINTH DAY

The stage of my life has changed; old doors are closed and new ones now stand open.

I dedicate the vigil for this day and night to the elders in whose homes I learned about the world.
And I think about the ways I want my home to be similar and the ways in which I want it to be different.

I honor this place that will shelter me, and I embrace the changes and opportunities that this move invites into my life.

THE TENTH DAY

The stage of my life has changed; old doors are closed and new ones now stand open.

Unpacking gives me further opportunity to discriminate. Now that I am here, what did I bring that doesn't fit? I continue the process of releasing the unnecessary by discarding, or passing on, that which I know will not serve me.

I honor this place that will shelter me, and I embrace the changes and opportunities that this move invites into my life.

THE ELEVENTH DAY

The stage of my life has changed; old doors are closed and new ones now stand open.

Releasing makes way for birth and gives me the chance to think about the new things I need to make this home reflect the beauty and harmony I hope to feel here.
I will take time to consider my new purchases and I will enjoy their selection and reflect on how they will fit into the character of my new home.

I honor this place that will shelter me, and I embrace the changes and opportunities that this move invites into my life.

THE TWELFTH DAY

The stage of my life has changed; old doors are closed and new ones now stand open.

I ask for guidance and protection within these walls and for the inner security I need to take the risks required to see my dreams come true.

I honor this place that will shelter me, and I embrace the changes and opportunities that this move invites into my life.

THE THIRTEENTH DAY

The stage of my life has changed; old doors are closed and new ones now stand open.

I direct my focus for today to the people around me who define the words "friends" and "family."
May my new setting be one where these relationships can deepen, the stories of our lives be shared, and the joy of our bond be savored.

I honor this place that will shelter me, and I embrace the changes and opportunities that this move invites into my life.

THE FOURTEENTH DAY

The stage of my life has changed; old doors are closed and new ones now stand open.

The way to this place is familiar now, and I can usually even remember my new zip code!
Changing places, changing worlds.
I am showing myself firsthand that I can change with grace and presence.

As I develop my ability to envision and reflect, I increase my flexibility and look forward to greater balance in my changes and transitions.

I honor this place that will shelter me, and I embrace the changes and opportunities that this move invites into my life.

THE FIFTEENTH DAY

The stage of my life has changed; old doors are closed and new ones now stand open.

Now that I have made it my own, I christen this place a safe harbor where I can heal in times of strife and renew in times of stress.
In all seasons, I can count on its protection.

I honor this place that will shelter me, and I embrace the changes and opportunities that this move invites into my life.

THE SIXTEENTH DAY

The stage of my life has changed; old doors are closed and new ones now stand open.

I take this moment to reflect on my surroundings.
The people and places that border this home—how do I feel
about them? And do I fit in? And do I care?
I am connected to everything around me and in this vigil I will
reflect to see if there are things I need to do to improve this
connection.

*I honor this place that will shelter me, and I embrace the changes
and opportunities that this move invites into my life.*

THE SEVENTEENTH DAY

*The stage of my life has changed; old doors are closed and new ones
now stand open.*

What would I like to see unfold for me during my time in this
home?
I will think today about my goals for the near and distant
future.
If this is my stage, what parts do I most want to play?

*I honor this place that will shelter me, and I embrace the changes
and opportunities that this move invites into my life.*

THE EIGHTEENTH DAY

The stage of my life has changed; old doors are closed and new ones now stand open.

I watch with interest as the familiar events and small rituals of my day now take shape in this new world.
How sweet this combination of old and new.

I honor this place that will shelter me, and I embrace the changes and opportunities that this move invites into my life.

THE NINETEENTH DAY

The stage of my life has changed; old doors are closed and new ones now stand open.

We all talk to ourselves inside our heads.
Am I using my new environment to create more positive dialogues between myself and me? To convey respect and patience?
New surroundings invite new ways of being, with ourselves and with others.

I honor this place that will shelter me, and I embrace the changes and opportunities that this move invites into my life.

THE TWENTIETH DAY

The stage of my life has changed; old doors are closed and new ones now stand open.

In this time of quiet focusing, I promise to add the small touches that remind me to celebrate a little every day—the music, the flowers, the postcard from someone dear displayed where it catches my eye.
In this spirit of celebration it is now time for me to say, to myself and to my new home, what is deepest in my heart:

....

I honor this place that will shelter me, and I embrace the changes and opportunities that this move invites into my life.

THE TWENTY-FIRST DAY

The stage of my life has changed; old doors are closed and new ones now stand open.

My vigils to embrace my new home draw to an end.
May the presence that has accompanied these readings invite a deep quality of poise into my world.

May my responses be fresh, may my insights be true, and may I walk with grace and optimism through all the changes that come my way.

I honor this place that will shelter me, and I embrace the changes and opportunities that this move invites into my life.

The End of a Relationship

ONE OF THE reasons it hurts so much when a relationship ends is that it begins in such joy and gladness. Even if the union was not formalized with marriage, still, it had its birth in hope and high spirits, with shared visions and plans. To be left alone in the shadow of disappointment and abandoned dreams feels so unfair when we reached for happiness with such optimism.

As a heart breaks it grasps at the extremes of emotion. Denial may prevail one day and despair the next. Anger and guilt trade places like a ball in endless volley, and it can seem impossible to find a place of stillness and safety. How can we carry on amid such turbulence and frustration?

Honesty can bring surprising relief. When you are, at last, able to speak honestly of your sorrow, you can open to the comfort of those who love you and to the guidance of the One whose love is unfailing. Why do we pretend we are not hurting and downplay the importance of this hurt? Whom do we think we are fooling? We risked and reached out for a partner who became the heart's own treasure, and now not only do we have to go through this pain alone, but the hurt, at its very core, stems from the one we loved.

Leaving and being left each has its own perspective, but it may be that the hurt is essentially the same. Our intellect might convince us that the decision to leave is necessary, but the heart can be far from sure as it misses the parts of the relationship that are rewarding and familiar. Uncertainty and guilt can torment us as we wonder if we are walking away from something we did not have the maturity and patience to make work.

In being left, we come face to face with betrayal, disillusionment, and defeat. Rejection threatens our self-esteem, and the fear of being alone can haunt us even though we may be surrounded with friends and activity.

In the midst of my own difficult parting, the world suddenly switched from color to black and white. It seemed that so much of my vitality was lost with the day-to-day restructuring of life, and this was tedious and depressing. I was also profoundly humbled. Just the year before, I had seemed to have most of the answers, and then, as I suffered this change, none of the answers made sense.

It was a long and painful winter. I carried on as best I could. I celebrated holidays with flat enthusiasm. I leaned on friends and family as much as possible without being a nuisance. My apartment alternated between compulsive order and complete chaos.

Finally, buds appeared on the trees, the air warmed, and life began its tentative rebirth. I was driving through the park with a friend one day and couldn't get over the beauty around me. I exclaimed that I hadn't remembered a spring this lovely in years. He looked at me with a smile and remarked, "You lived"—and he was right. I had survived a dark winter and a long journey of hurt and uncertainty and while I might not have had all the answers again, I was on my way. The color was back.

No matter what kind of face you wear in public, this is a time when you hurt. You need to know that this is normal and healthy. Give your tears the respect and freedom they deserve, for they offer comfort and release. Listen to the stories of those around you. We have all been hurt and this painful truth can be a reassuring reminder that even though you may feel that you are alone, you are not. Others have survived this passage and can share counsel and consolation.

Listen to your own stories and allow the honesty they provide to guide and direct you. The vigils to ease the ending of a relationship are intended to put you in touch with these stories. As you enter into their spirit of quiet presence, you affirm your willingness to heal and to hope again.

THE FIRST DAY

The bond that has held my heart and my hopes is broken, and I ask for the guidance to release the past and renew my life.

I am hurt, angry, and confused und disappointed, more than I can say.
Tears of rage and hopelessness wash through me and the future has lost definition.

I have many challenges, and the greatest one is to discover who I am. I respect my search for this knowledge and trust it to bring assurance and resolution.

THE SECOND DAY

The bond that has held my heart and my hopes is broken, and I ask for the guidance to release the past and renew my life.

My emotions are running wild, and peaceful moments are short-lived.

The inner chaos is as uncomfortable as the idea of being alone again.

I need to acknowledge both these feelings and the opportunity to be aware of them, knowing that honesty leads to balance.

I have many challenges, and the greatest one is to discover who I am. I respect my search for this knowledge and trust it to bring assurance and resolution.

THE THIRD DAY

The bond that has held my heart and my hopes is broken, and I ask for the guidance to release the past and renew my life.

I am angry about so much as I strive to sort through my grievances.

It is too soon to release that anger, so I will hold it as skillfully as I can, using its force to carry me on to the choices and decisions that ask for my attention.

I have many challenges, and the greatest one is to discover who I am. I respect my search for this knowledge and trust it to bring assurance and resolution.

THE FOURTH DAY

The bond that has held my heart and my hopes is broken, and I ask for the guidance to release the past and renew my life.

My memory is vulnerable and it is easy to miss the familiarity and comfort of "us" and the sense that we belonged together. I reach for the clarity to understand why this painful change is necessary.

I have many challenges, and the greatest one is to discover who I am. I respect my search for this knowledge and trust it to bring assurance and resolution.

THE FIFTH DAY

The bond that has held my heart and my hopes is broken, and I ask for the guidance to release the past and renew my life.

Just beyond my anger and sorrow is a field of regret.
If only this had happened instead of that. If I had made different choices, would we still be together?
As I gradually forgive myself and the one I have loved I will be able to transform these regrets into understanding.

I have many challenges, and the greatest one is to discover who I am. I respect my search for this knowledge and trust it to bring assurance and resolution.

THE SIXTH DAY

The bond that has held my heart and my hopes is broken, and I ask for the guidance to release the past and renew my life.

Most changes unfold gradually, yet this one seems so abrupt. I may have had doubts about our being together, but suddenly the worst has happened.
I will trust the rhythm of days and nights as they pass to remind me that time brings healing and acceptance.

I have many challenges, and the greatest one is to discover who I am. I respect my search for this knowledge and trust it to bring assurance and resolution.

THE SEVENTH DAY

The bond that has held my heart and my hopes is broken, and I ask for the guidance to release the past and renew my life.

Intimacy moves through a relationship in silent and powerful ways and calls to memory in a language all its own.

The intimacy we shared amplifies this hurt and I am reminded to hold these private feelings with respect, and to extend a gentle understanding to the parts of me that remain sensitive to these memories.

I have many challenges, and the greatest one is to discover who I am. I respect my search for this knowledge and trust it to bring assurance and resolution.

THE EIGHTH DAY

The bond that has held my heart and my hopes is broken, and I ask for the guidance to release the past and renew my life.

It takes so much time, effort, and emotion to tend a strained relationship. Are there friends and family that I have neglected? What interests were pushed aside as I put this relationship first?

Although I may be hurting, I am now free to contemplate the many possibilities life offers.

I have many challenges, and the greatest one is to discover who I am. I respect my search for this knowledge and trust it to bring assurance and resolution.

THE NINTH DAY

The bond that has held my heart and my hopes is broken, and I ask for the guidance to release the past and renew my life.

I was comfortable in the security a partnership provides, and now I often feel tentative and unsure.
Humility can be a connection to wonder as it cuts through complicated ways of thinking and responding and leaves us open to experience the world from a different perspective.
Now I have the chance to refresh my outlook and to make new beginnings.

I have many challenges, and the greatest one is to discover who I am. I respect my search for this knowledge and trust it to bring assurance and resolution.

THE TENTH DAY

The bond that has held my heart and my hopes is broken, and I ask for the guidance to release the past and renew my life.

Each time I describe what has taken place, I reach to cover my hurt with words.

I feel embarrassed and vulnerable.

The people in my life deserve a response to their concern, but I have the right to decide just how much I feel comfortable revealing and to whom.

I have many challenges, and the greatest one is to discover who I am. I respect my search for this knowledge and trust it to bring assurance and resolution.

THE ELEVENTH DAY

The bond that has held my heart and my hopes is broken, and I ask for the guidance to release the past and renew my life.

This is a time when some friends will be approving, others disapproving—and everyone will have advice.

Perhaps it is a time for me to reflect on how much the approval of others influences my decisions.

I must choose my confidants with care and guard against letting the confusion and resentments of others become my own.

I know that there is One I can always trust.

I have many challenges, and the greatest one is to discover who I am. I respect my search for this knowledge and trust it to bring assurance and resolution.

THE TWELFTH DAY

The bond that has held my heart and my hopes is broken, and I ask for the guidance to release the past and renew my life.

Taking my anger out on those close to me is not an answer to my pain. I need to remember that there are healthier outlets for anger—a brisk walk, a hot bath, a task that needs a full measure of energy and attention.

As I find safe ways to release my anger, acceptance can take its place.

I have many challenges, and the greatest one is to discover who I am. I respect my search for this knowledge and trust it to bring assurance and resolution.

THE THIRTEENTH DAY

The bond that has held my heart and my hopes is broken, and I ask for the guidance to release the past and renew my life.

It is natural to look for places to shoot my arrows of blame. Some land squarely on my judgments about the one who is gone and others inflict their pain on parts of me that are the most tender.

I will try to understand that I can learn more from responsibility than from blame. To work honestly through my anger is to release the need to blame.

I have many challenges, and the greatest one is to discover who I am. I respect my search for this knowledge and trust it to bring assurance and resolution.

THE FOURTEENTH DAY

The bond that has held my heart and my hopes is broken, and I ask for the guidance to release the past and renew my life.

I need to acknowledge that this relationship was necessary, that it carried me and someone I loved deeply to realms of discovery, joy, and trust.

That it was unable to withstand all the challenges, changes, and conflicts should not diminish its value.

I have many challenges, and the greatest one is to discover who I am. I respect my search for this knowledge and trust it to bring assurance and resolution.

THE FIFTEENTH DAY

The bond that has held my heart and my hopes is broken, and I ask for the guidance to release the past and renew my life.

Even though my relationship has failed, this doesn't mean that I am a failure.
It is helpful to remember the many things I do well and the qualities that make me glad to be me.
It is helpful to remember that my relationship with God can never fail.
I am discouraged, heartbroken, and wounded, but I am also resilient. As I recommit to my strengths and renew my faith, I am able to see the path through this change with greater clarity and confidence.

I have many challenges, and the greatest one is to discover who I am. I respect my search for this knowledge and trust it to bring assurance and resolution.

THE SIXTEENTH DAY

The bond that has held my heart and my hopes is broken, and I ask for the guidance to release the past and renew my life.

Even in my sadness I know that life goes on, and I use that going on as an affirmation of hope and possibility.
Sometimes the small details of living can provide comforting ritual and a familiar pattern to hold me safely until I have healed enough to risk again.

I have many challenges, and the greatest one is to discover who I am. I respect my search for this knowledge and trust it to bring assurance and resolution.

THE SEVENTEENTH DAY

The bond that has held my heart and my hopes is broken, and I ask for the guidance to release the past and renew my life.

I struggle to find a new way to relate to someone who was once a friend and lover, someone who now seems distant and strange.
Our communication about the decisions we must make to-

gether concerning the ending of our relationship can be strained and difficult.

I will try not to misconstrue what is said.

I ask for the patience and dignity to make my needs clear while respecting, as best I can, the other point of view.

I have many challenges, and the greatest one is to discover who I am. I respect my search for this knowledge and trust it to bring assurance and resolution.

THE EIGHTEENTH DAY

The bond that has held my heart and my hopes is broken, and I ask for the guidance to release the past and renew my life.

There are levels of feeling that I must pass through, but I can set my own rhythm and pace for accepting and integrating this change.

I need to remember that rushing into a new relationship may bring complications I will regret.

I need to remember my right to say no.

I have many challenges, and the greatest one is to discover who I am. I respect my search for this knowledge and trust it to bring assurance and resolution.

THE NINETEENTH DAY

The bond that has held my heart and my hopes is broken, and I ask for the guidance to release the past and renew my life.

I seek the guidance to honor my hurt and disappointment without getting lost in it. Bitterness is not a good long-term friend.
A healthy balance of quiet and activity, of understanding and discipline, can carry me safely through this season of emotional unrest.

I have many challenges, and the greatest one is to discover who I am. I respect my search for this knowledge and trust it to bring assurance and resolution.

THE TWENTIETH DAY

The bond that has held my heart and my hopes is broken, and I ask for the guidance to release the past and renew my life.

Sooner or later I have to consider the idea of letting go, not only of this relationship, but of the angst as well.
A deep sigh now and then can signal to my emotional body

that it does not have to carry this pain forever.

Although I cannot choose my feelings, I can, with prayer and trust, be more in control of my response to them.

I have many challenges, and the greatest one is to discover who I am. I respect my search for this knowledge and trust it to bring assurance and resolution.

THE TWENTY-FIRST DAY

The bond that has held my heart and my hopes is broken, and I ask for the guidance to release the past and renew my life.

Through this time of pain and confusion I need to remember the value of laughter and play and the magic of "mental vacations."

These imaginary excursions provide ways to see and feel myself in places where I thrive and to imagine my heart mended and my life filled with happiness again.

I have many challenges, and the greatest one is to discover who I am. I respect my search for this knowledge and trust it to bring assurance and resolution.

THE TWENTY-SECOND DAY

The bond that has held my heart and my hopes is broken, and I ask
for the guidance to release the past and renew my life.

Perhaps this is a good time to reflect upon changes I need to
make in the way I look at a relationship and what it can and
cannot provide.
It cannot change an unhappy childhood. It is probably not the
road to financial security. It can't guarantee that my shortcomings will no longer matter.
Hopeful but realistic expectations enable me to form a roman-
tic partnership with maturity when I am ready to share that
partnership again.

I have many challenges, and the greatest one is to discover who I
am. I respect my search for this knowledge and trust it to bring
assurance and resolution.

THE TWENTY-THIRD DAY

The bond that has held my heart and my hopes is broken, and I ask
for the guidance to release the past and renew my life.

The loneliness inside a relationship that was no longer alive can hold such emptiness and despair.
Although I sometimes ache for the lost familiar, I am beginning now to open to new life and admit to its possibility.

I have many challenges, and the greatest one is to discover who I am. I respect my search for this knowledge and trust it to bring assurance and resolution.

THE TWENTY-FOURTH DAY

The bond that has held my heart and my hopes is broken, and I ask for the guidance to release the past and renew my life.

Resentment holds us back in dark and powerful ways.
It can make me a slave to my own anger and hurt.
It can keep me chained to people and ideas I most need to release.

I have many challenges, and the greatest one is to discover who I am. I respect my search for this knowledge and trust it to bring assurance and resolution.

THE TWENTY-FIFTH DAY

The bond that has held my heart and my hopes is broken, and I ask for the guidance to release the past and renew my life.

To forgive is to understand that we do the best we can according to our abilities and maturity.
To forgive is to be gentle with our humanness.
To forgive is to open to the grace and the heart of the One.

I have many challenges, and the greatest one is to discover who I am. I respect my search for this knowledge and trust it to bring assurance and resolution.

THE TWENTY-SIXTH DAY

The bond that has held my heart and my hopes is broken, and I ask for the guidance to release the past and renew my life.

It is time now for me to say, in my own words, what is deepest in my heart:

....

I have many challenges, and the greatest one is to discover who I am. I respect my search for this knowledge and trust it to bring assurance and resolution.

THE TWENTY-SEVENTH DAY

The bond that has held my heart and my hopes is broken, and I ask for the guidance to release the past and renew my life.

I see now with some objectivity the strengths and shortcomings of this union that has ended.
To walk away without these insights is to leave treasures behind that are rightfully mine.
Honest evaluation of my part in this sadness can show me changes I need to make in my thoughts, my actions, and my heart.

I have many challenges, and the greatest one is to discover who I am. I respect my search for this knowledge and trust it to bring assurance and resolution.

THE TWENTY-EIGHTH DAY

The bond that has held my heart and my hopes is broken, and I ask for the guidance to release the past and renew my life.

Thoughts provide patterns for reality. A thought has a life and vitality of its own. As I withdraw energy from judgmental thoughts about the one who is gone and about myself, I create a pattern for my own release.

May the hurts and lessons of these times dissolve into my soul as new strength.

May my capacity to love and trust be deepened.

May I be blessed with the courage, the patience, and the understanding to complete this journey in a way that will bring honor to my spirit.

I have many challenges, and the greatest one is to discover who I am. I respect my search for this knowledge and trust it to bring assurance and resolution.

The Loss of a Job

WHAT WE DO for a living says so much about who we are, to others and to ourselves, that when our occupational identity is in flux or crisis, we often become uncertain about everything else. Without the familiar pattern and security of our work, a general uneasiness can settle over our lives.

This time of change, however, need not be without its gifts. Losing the well-worn routine that hurries us along provides a chance to consider the many ways our work shapes our sense of self. Without the opportunity to step back and review this relationship, we may believe that we *are* our work. We forget to ask important questions about how our career fits into the larger definition of ourselves. During a job transition, we have the advantage of standing in a place where new choices are possible, even necessary.

This is a moment for honesty rather than despair. It is a time to inquire about what kinds of activity fill us with purpose and the feeling that our contribution is important. Does our work add to our life's hopes and pleasures, or is it a distraction? How can we find work that expands and enriches us?

When my son lost his job recently, I asked him what bothered him the most and he replied, "the loss of freedom." We don't usually think of our jobs in terms of freedom, especially on days when we would rather be at the beach, but the liberation he felt doing something he enjoyed was as appreciated as the economic freedom brought by his weekly pay.

This loss of freedom, though uncomfortable and disconcerting, can encourage us to become acquainted with ourselves in an entirely different way. Being released from a professional identity can prompt us to look beyond immediate needs and think about how we truly want to spend the many hours that make up our world of work.

These vigils offer focus and reassurance during this important transition. Their observance is an invitation to look for the opportunity in adversity and accept this challenge with grace and determination.

THE FIRST DAY

The world of my work is changing, and my professional identity, direction, and security are unsettled.

The routine of my work life has been a cornerstone, and it is hard to believe that this is happening.
Even when things were difficult and I longed to be somewhere else, I valued the continuity, recognition, and familiarity that my work provided.

As one form dissolves, another takes its place. My work now is to seek and to recognize a new form that will provide the opportunity for growth and reward.

THE SECOND DAY

The world of my work is changing, and my professional identity, direction, and security are unsettled.

Part of me is racing to come up with a plan, and another part is confused and unfocused.

The part I am trying to ignore is simply terrified. Just thinking of the process that lies ahead is exhausting.

In facing the unknown, I need to accept my fear and disillusionment with patience.

As one form dissolves, another takes its place. My work now is to seek and to recognize a new form that will provide the opportunity for growth and reward.

THE THIRD DAY

The world of my work is changing, and my professional identity, direction, and security are unsettled.

I feel guilt, anger, and a haunting sense of not belonging.

I need to remember what I know about grieving and realize that it will take time to accept these feelings.

As one form dissolves, another takes its place. My work now is to seek and to recognize a new form that will provide the opportunity for growth and reward.

THE FOURTH DAY

The world of my work is changing, and my professional identity, direction, and security are unsettled.

Acknowledging my feelings is one thing, but judging them is another.
This is not the time to examine my character flaws.
I need encouragement and reassurance from those around me and from myself.

As one form dissolves, another takes its place. My work now is to seek and to recognize a new form that will provide the opportunity for growth and reward.

THE FIFTH DAY

The world of my work is changing, and my professional identity, direction, and security are unsettled.

When I feel disconnected and lost, let me remember the ways in which other people value me and the places where I belong.
I am capable. I am respected. I am effective.

As one form dissolves, another takes its place. My work now is to seek and to recognize a new form that will provide the opportunity for growth and reward.

THE SIXTH DAY

The world of my work is changing, and my professional identity, direction, and security are unsettled.

It is discouraging to think of all the time and effort I have invested.
It seems like a sacrifice.
Perhaps I can begin to understand the original meaning of the word: "to make sacred."
Perhaps this is a sacred passage in which my insecurity is sacrificed for trust in whatever is to come.

As one form dissolves, another takes its place. My work now is to seek and to recognize a new form that will provide the opportunity for growth and reward.

THE SEVENTH DAY

The world of my work is changing, and my professional identity, direction, and security are unsettled.

The unknown can be intimidating, but it can be exciting, too.
To a great extent, the choice is mine.
As I trust the One Life for my direction and security I am reminded that the spirit thrives on adventure.

As one form dissolves, another takes its place. My work now is to seek and to recognize a new form that will provide the opportunity for growth and reward.

THE EIGHTH DAY

The world of my work is changing, and my professional identity, direction, and security are unsettled.

This may be a financially difficult time.
Let me remember that wealth has little to do with what I have, but instead depends on how I appreciate and enjoy it.

As one form dissolves, another takes its place. My work now is to seek and to recognize a new form that will provide the opportunity for growth and reward.

THE NINTH DAY

The world of my work is changing, and my professional identity, direction, and security are unsettled.

One of the things that sweeping change presents is the gift of an open field.
Usually life seems very predictable and now there is a big question mark.
Let me take this opportunity to reexamine ideas and possibilities that earlier seemed like unrealistic dreams.
Do they have new meaning in light of what has happened?

As one form dissolves, another takes its place. My work now is to seek and to recognize a new form that will provide the opportunity for growth and reward.

THE TENTH DAY

The world of my work is changing, and my professional identity, direction, and security are unsettled.

As I explore new options I will need to listen to what my body knows.

The way an environment feels can tell me a great deal about how I might fit in.
I must be careful not to grasp at something just to fill the gap.
I will observe when I feel tense and uncomfortable and wait until I am at ease.

As one form dissolves, another takes its place. My work now is to seek and to recognize a new form that will provide the opportunity for growth and reward.

THE ELEVENTH DAY

The world of my work is changing, and my professional identity, direction, and security are unsettled.

In trying to hold pain and helplessness at bay, we sometimes retreat into the shadows.
At times this may be healing, but eventually it can freeze my response to new ideas and cause me to overlook opportunities.
As I embrace the pleasure of my favorite activities, I affirm

that even through the most difficult parts of this change, I deserve to enjoy my life.

As one form dissolves, another takes its place. My work now is to seek and to recognize a new form that will provide the opportunity for growth and reward.

THE TWELFTH DAY

The world of my work is changing, and my professional identity, direction, and security are unsettled.

All the roads from here seem to be dead ends.
I am unsure of the next step and sometimes it is as though there is no next step.
I may not consider myself artistic, but I have talents that allow me to create in my own way.
To paint, to build, to cook, to write, to plant—to express myself in these ways can rekindle the flame of new perspective.

As one form dissolves, another takes its place. My work now is to seek and to recognize a new form that will provide the opportunity for growth and reward.

THE THIRTEENTH DAY

The world of my work is changing, and my professional identity, direction, and security are unsettled.

It may not be easy to observe the disciplines of my life in the face of this disruption.

When the temptation arises to miss just this once, I will remember why I took up these practices in the first place and realize that I must be willing to follow through with the necessary patience and faithfulness.

Rather than berate myself when I lapse, may I remember the welcome that awaits me when I come home to my promises.

As one form dissolves, another takes its place. My work now is to seek and to recognize a new form that will provide the opportunity for growth and reward.

THE FOURTEENTH DAY

The world of my work is changing, and my professional identity, direction, and security are unsettled.

I am reminded that my beliefs color and perhaps even create my world. Am I able to recognize the ones that have grown stale?

As I seek a new context for my work, I need to pay attention to self-limiting beliefs.
I need to remember that in God, all things are possible.

As one form dissolves, another takes its place. My work now is to seek and to recognize a new form that will provide the opportunity for growth and reward.

THE FIFTEENTH DAY

The world of my work is changing, and my professional identity, direction, and security are unsettled.

It can feel good to put something in order—clean out a closet, sort through a sock drawer, organize a bookshelf, or tackle the back porch.
Bringing order to the small corners of my life lends a reassuring sense of command and reminds me of the pleasure in small triumphs.

As one form dissolves, another takes its place. My work now is to seek and to recognize a new form that will provide the opportunity for growth and reward.

THE SIXTEENTH DAY

The world of my work is changing, and my professional identity, direction, and security are unsettled.

Resourcefulness is an important ally in times of change and transition, and sometimes it needs to be coaxed by recalling solutions I have found to problems in the past.
Resourcefulness means being awake to unusual and unexpected options. It means thinking in the present tense and honoring my ingenuity to find ways around obstacles.

As one form dissolves, another takes its place. My work now is to seek and to recognize a new form that will provide the opportunity for growth and reward.

THE SEVENTEENTH DAY

The world of my work is changing, and my professional identity, direction, and security are unsettled.

This is a time to talk to everyone—friends, acquaintances, family.
It doesn't matter if it is called networking, advertising, or fishing.
The people in my life may have surprising resources, connec-

tions, and ideas, and I resolve to engage their response ener-
getically.

*As one form dissolves, another takes its place. My work now is to
seek and to recognize a new form that will provide the opportunity
for growth and reward.*

THE EIGHTEENTH DAY

*The world of my work is changing, and my professional identity,
direction, and security are unsettled.*

Rejection seems to be an unavoidable part of this process and
with it, times of sullen disappointment.
It helps to remember that guidance takes many forms, and
sometimes an unanswered prayer can be a blessing in disguise.

*As one form dissolves, another takes its place. My work now is to
seek and to recognize a new form that will provide the opportunity
for growth and reward.*

THE NINETEENTH DAY

*The world of my work is changing, and my professional identity,
direction, and security are unsettled.*

Am I approaching this search with an appreciation of my best qualities?

The foundation of resilience is optimism and the ability to focus on the positive in myself and my circumstance.

As one form dissolves, another takes its place. My work now is to seek and to recognize a new form that will provide the opportunity for growth and reward.

THE TWENTIETH DAY

The world of my work is changing, and my professional identity, direction, and security are unsettled.

Am I giving thought to who I am *now*?

Am I defining myself by old boundaries and trying to fit today's "me" into yesterday's career needs?

Acknowledging my achievement enables me to express it to others, and this helps to provide the clarity I need to navigate this change with confidence.

As one form dissolves, another takes its place. My work now is to seek and to recognize a new form that will provide the opportunity for growth and reward.

THE TWENTY-FIRST DAY

The world of my work is changing, and my professional identity, direction, and security are unsettled.

How have these times of challenge and uncertainty reverberated through the lives of those close to me?
Have I been so caught up in the details and demands of this passage that I have failed to address their concerns?
Have I forgotten how much the heart welcomes words of reassurance and appreciation?

As one form dissolves, another takes its place. My work now is to seek and to recognize a new form that will provide the opportunity for growth and reward.

THE TWENTY-SECOND DAY

The world of my work is changing, and my professional identity, direction, and security are unsettled.

The Chinese character for the word "crisis" is a combination of the symbols for danger and opportunity.
Though danger may not actually be present, uncertainty can feel that way.

As I focus on this opportunity, I trust in my ability to remain positive and receptive to new ideas.

As one form dissolves, another takes its place. My work now is to seek and to recognize a new form that will provide the opportunity for growth and reward.

THE TWENTY-THIRD DAY

The world of my work is changing, and my professional identity, direction, and security are unsettled.

There are days when I feel like hiding in the hope that everything will be different tomorrow, but the truth is that I have to *make* it different.
One thing leads to another, and exploring every option every day builds a momentum that can carry me successfully over the threshold of this change.

As one form dissolves, another takes its place. My work now is to seek and to recognize a new form that will provide the opportunity for growth and reward.

THE TWENTY-FOURTH DAY

The world of my work is changing, and my professional identity, direction, and security are unsettled.

Sometimes it is necessary to go backward in order to go forward, much like reversing the car from the driveway in order to proceed on one's way.

Musicians practice scales daily, acrobats warm up using simple combinations, and athletes sometimes revert to basic maneuvers to achieve a victory.

Understanding this principle can alleviate despair when it feels as though my forward motion is in jeopardy.

As one form dissolves, another takes its place. My work now is to seek and to recognize a new form that will provide the opportunity for growth and reward.

THE TWENTY-FIFTH DAY

The world of my work is changing, and my professional identity, direction, and security are unsettled.

So much about this transition can be intimidating.
It is tempting to feel that I do not have the skills or ability to reach as high as I would like.
While it may be true that I need to consider additional study or training, I must also recognize that my own experiences can provide surprising credentials.

As one form dissolves, another takes its place. My work now is to seek and to recognize a new form that will provide the opportunity for growth and reward.

THE TWENTY-SIXTH DAY

The world of my work is changing, and my professional identity, direction, and security are unsettled.

It is time now to say, in my own words, what is deepest in my heart:

....

As one form dissolves, another takes its place. My work now is to seek and to recognize a new form that will provide the opportunity for growth and reward.

THE TWENTY-SEVENTH DAY

*The world of my work is changing, and my professional identity,
direction, and security are unsettled.*

When this journey grows long, the natural world can offer
solace.
To gaze at the stars is to remember what vast really means.
It is important to celebrate the passing of a season and to
envision my success in the next one.
It is healing to realize that all things unfold in their own time.

*As one form dissolves, another takes its place. My work now is to
seek and to recognize a new form that will provide the opportunity
for growth and reward.*

THE TWENTY-EIGHTH DAY

*The world of my work is changing, and my professional identity,
direction, and security are unsettled.*

Humor and originality are valuable allies on this treasure
hunt. Their gifts bring inventiveness and a light heart.
They enable me to trust my instincts and rely on the Source
of all blessings.

They remind me to look beyond "work" to "vocation" and to know that as I search for this vocation, it searches, also, for me.

As one form dissolves, another takes its place. My work now is to seek and to recognize a new form that will provide the opportunity for growth and reward.

A Child Leaving Home

WE SPEND SO much time preparing our children to leave home and assume their place in the world, but we spend very little time preparing ourselves. With their departure our priorities change, our identities shift, and we are forced to admit that we are growing older. We look for new ways of nurturing and try to find the balance between too much or too little involvement in our grown children's lives.

My son will be leaving home soon, and the tears come easily. With a full, rewarding life of my own, I wonder how I can be so emotional about this. I know it is a new beginning for me as well as for him. I think about the time I will have for long-abandoned projects and mentally redecorate his room. I wonder who will assume the roles he's managed for years, from garbage detail to fish-tank maintenance, and who will make the old piano sing?

How is it possible that the daily joys and struggles of being a parent to this particular young person are over? As long as our children are just down the hall, it seems as if we can still impart one last instruction or share a profound discovery. But at this stage they are listening more to their future and less to us.

These vigils provide an opportunity to speak about our concerns and articulate the maze of feelings that struggle for expression. As we quiet our hearts we can begin to honor this moment as a commencement, an ending that is also a beginning, for our child and for ourselves.

THE FIRST DAY

My child, you leave my home but not my heart.

There is so much to feel about this change.
You still seem so young, and I wonder how it will be for you
once you are on your own.
I wonder how it will be for me as your life takes shape apart
from mine.

Your years in my care have blessed me as I have watched the
unfolding of your life. It is with pride and tenderness that I now
release that life to follow its own promise. I love you. I believe in
you. I wish only the best for you.

THE SECOND DAY

My child, you leave my home but not my heart.

I cannot help but be amazed that the years of your childhood
have passed so quickly.

I nurtured your first steps with patience, and cheered for your independence. Now I pray that you will discover these qualities as you take your first steps into this new life.

Your years in my care have blessed me as I have watched the unfolding of your life. It is with pride and tenderness that I now release that life to follow its own promise. I love you. I believe in you. I wish only the best for you.

THE THIRD DAY

My child, you leave my home but not my heart.

We each have so much on our minds as this change takes form, and our concerns and agendas are very different. Along with the right to your own focus and vision, I add the gift of my understanding.

Your years in my care have blessed me as I have watched the unfolding of your life. It is with pride and tenderness that I now release that life to follow its own promise. I love you. I believe in you. I wish only the best for you.

THE FOURTH DAY

My child, you leave my home but not my heart.

My memories can serve as guides.
I need to reach back to see how those who raised me blessed my own leave-taking, and where their attitudes made it uncomfortable and difficult.
I need to remember what it is like to have one foot in the familiar and another in the unknown.

Your years in my care have blessed me as I have watched the unfolding of your life. It is with pride and tenderness that I now release that life to follow its own promise. I love you. I believe in you. I wish only the best for you.

THE FIFTH DAY

My child, you leave my home but not my heart.

It seems like yesterday that your world was mended with my touch.
The crises and traumas of your growing up were held at bay as I wielded parental power in defense of your well-being.

How helpless I feel now that this role is no longer mine.
How comforting to remember that the One Spirit protects
you now as you embark on your life and set off to realize your
dreams.

Your years in my care have blessed me as I have watched the
unfolding of your life. It is with pride and tenderness that I now
release that life to follow its own promise. I love you. I believe in
you. I wish only the best for you.

THE SIXTH DAY

My child, you leave my home but not my heart.

As with any loss, there is a need to grieve, to say good-bye in
ways private and dear.
You are leaving my home, not my life—but our relationship
will never be quite the same.
I feel uncomfortable expressing these feelings to you as you
happily prepare to take your leave. I will find other times and
places for these emotions, allowing them their honesty and
poignancy.

Your years in my care have blessed me as I have watched the
unfolding of your life. It is with pride and tenderness that I now

release that life to follow its own promise. I love you. I believe in you. I wish only the best for you.

THE SEVENTH DAY

My child, you leave my home but not my heart.

Our endings color our beginnings.
May this ending celebrate our years of love and learning together and be a time to let go of disagreements, resentments, and patterns that stand in the way of our new beginnings.

Your years in my care have blessed me as I have watched the unfolding of your life. It is with pride and tenderness that I now release that life to follow its own promise. I love you. I believe in you. I wish only the best for you.

THE EIGHTH DAY

My child, you leave my home but not my heart.

Sometimes I feel you have little understanding of the sacrifices and challenges of being a parent, and I admit that I never thought about these things when I was growing up.
There are times when I do not feel as appreciated as I would like.

The qualities needed to feel gratitude and express appreciation grow with the years.

I can remember to appreciate myself as a parent and to share that acknowledgment with those who have helped to teach, love, and guide you.

Your years in my care have blessed me as I have watched the unfolding of your life. It is with pride and tenderness that I now release that life to follow its own promise. I love you. I believe in you. I wish only the best for you.

THE NINTH DAY

My child, you leave my home but not my heart.

Often I see myself in you, in your gestures or the way you move.

I am proud that part of me will be accompanying you and feel honored to be part of one generation expanding into the next.

Your years in my care have blessed me as I have watched the unfolding of your life. It is with pride and tenderness that I now release that life to follow its own promise. I love you. I believe in you. I wish only the best for you.

THE TENTH DAY

My child, you leave my home but not my heart.

Although I notice our resemblance and similar traits, I know
that this is a time when you are concerned about becoming
your own person, apart from your family and your childhood.
As I allow and encourage your freedom to define yourself and
what's important to you, let me provide the space for a new
relationship to develop between us.

*Your years in my care have blessed me as I have watched the
unfolding of your life. It is with pride and tenderness that I now
release that life to follow its own promise. I love you. I believe in
you. I wish only the best for you.*

THE ELEVENTH DAY

My child, you leave my home, but not my heart.

You must find ways to let me know how much or how little
you want me to be involved in your life.
I understand the value of comfort and reassurance, and will
look for the right time to voice comments, suggestions, and
advice.

I will remember that the best time to offer counsel is when you ask.

Your years in my care have blessed me as I have watched the unfolding of your life. It is with pride and tenderness that I now release that life to follow its own promise. I love you. I believe in you. I wish only the best for you.

THE TWELFTH DAY

My child, you leave my home, but not my heart.

When you were a baby I listened for your cry. As you grew older, I listened for your key in the door.
Through the years, I have grown good at listening, and I hope to grow better still.
I will listen to your stories and remember that a faithful listener hears secrets others overlook.

Your years in my care have blessed me as I have watched the unfolding of your life. It is with pride and tenderness that I now release that life to follow its own promise. I love you. I believe in you. I wish only the best for you.

THE THIRTEENTH DAY

My child, you leave my home but not my heart.

I will miss those parts of your life that have overlapped mine—your activities, your friends, the lights left on, the music from your room.
I have wished so often for moments of peace and quiet.
Now I wish for graceful adjustment to the stillness you leave behind.

Your years in my care have blessed me as I have watched the unfolding of your life. It is with pride and tenderness that I now release that life to follow its own promise. I love you. I believe in you. I wish only the best for you.

THE FOURTEENTH DAY

My child, you leave my home but not my heart.

I look back on our holidays and celebrations together and savor the gift of their memories.
May the spirit in which we shared the traditions of our family guide you to your own observance of the special times and days in your life.

Your years in my care have blessed me as I have watched the unfolding of your life. It is with pride and tenderness that I now release that life to follow its own promise. I love you. I believe in you. I wish only the best for you.

THE FIFTEENTH DAY

My child, you leave my home but not my heart.

So many of my own decisions and choices have been shaped by your needs.
It is intriguing to think of life without these boundaries and to stretch into the freedom this change allows.

Your years in my care have blessed me as I have watched the unfolding of your life. It is with pride and tenderness that I now release that life to follow its own promise. I love you. I believe in you. I wish only the best for you.

THE SIXTEENTH DAY

My child, you leave my home but not my heart.

I say each day that I wish only the best for you, but all life has its share of difficulty and pain.

So along with wishing you only the best, I also long for you to understand that hardship builds strength and confidence. May you come to know the difference between a real opportunity and a chimera.

May you respect adversity as teacher and guide and respect yourself as equal to your challenges.

Your years in my care have blessed me as I have watched the unfolding of your life. It is with pride and tenderness that I now release that life to follow its own promise. I love you. I believe in you. I wish only the best for you.

THE SEVENTEENTH DAY

My child, you leave my home but not my heart.

Your leaving raises questions about my relationships with those around me. To what do I need to attend?

As I redefine my role as parent, I will examine other roles in my life to see if they too need revision and try to discover who might be grateful for extra attention and affection.

Your years in my care have blessed me as I have watched the unfolding of your life. It is with pride and tenderness that I now

release that life to follow its own promise. I love you. I believe in you. I wish only the best for you.

THE EIGHTEENTH DAY

My child, you leave my home, but not my heart.

How can I relinquish the guilt I feel about mistakes I made as you were growing up?
It seems there are many things I would have handled differently.
I need to release my judgments and remember that acceptance and forgiveness make good companions as I travel on.

Your years in my care have blessed me as I have watched the unfolding of your life. It is with pride and tenderness that I now release that life to follow its own promise. I love you. I believe in you. I wish only the best for you.

THE NINETEENTH DAY

My child, you leave my home, but not my heart.

This home has been a place of safety for you and holds memories and connections to family.

After you leave here, changes will inevitably occur.
I will try to be sensitive about when and how I make these changes, and allow time for you to call your new surroundings home.

Your years in my care have blessed me as I have watched the unfolding of your life. It is with pride and tenderness that I now release that life to follow its own promise. I love you. I believe in you. I wish only the best for you.

THE TWENTIETH DAY

My child, you leave my home but not my heart.

As I focus on my gratitude for our years together, let me release feelings of emptiness and uncertainty about the shape of my life without you here.
Raising you developed my courage and maturity, and now letting you go can do the same.

Your years in my care have blessed me as I have watched the unfolding of your life. It is with pride and tenderness that I now release that life to follow its own promise. I love you. I believe in you. I wish only the best for you.

THE TWENTY-FIRST DAY

My child, you leave my home but not my heart.

It is easy to get lost in regrets, second thoughts, and concerns for the future, both yours and mine, but I also need to remember to feel proud and satisfied.

There is a certain peace in knowing that this part of a long and complicated process has reached completion.

Your years in my care have blessed me as I have watched the unfolding of your life. It is with pride and tenderness that I now release that life to follow its own promise. I love you. I believe in you. I wish only the best for you.

THE TWENTY-SECOND DAY

My child, you leave my home but not my heart.

This may be a good time to vary my routine—take a different way home, listen to music from another land, call a friend who leads an unusual life.

Doing familiar things in different ways can lead to interesting discoveries about the things I thought I knew.

Your years in my care have blessed me as I have watched the unfolding of your life. It is with pride and tenderness that I now release that life to follow its own promise. I love you. I believe in you. I wish only the best for you.

THE TWENTY-THIRD DAY

My child, you leave my home but not my heart.

One of the best gifts I can give you is a whole and healthy me.
I look for activities and interests that will ensure this.
My responsibility to provide a good example for you does not stop now.

Your years in my care have blessed me as I have watched the unfolding of your life. It is with pride and tenderness that I now release that life to follow its own promise. I love you. I believe in you. I wish only the best for you.

THE TWENTY-FOURTH DAY

My child, you leave my home but not my heart.

Just as I hope you will take the spirit of our holidays and celebrations with you, I'll be looking for ways to keep that spirit alive as my family at home grows smaller.

To celebrate, to worship, to observe the holidays, and to offer thanks is a pledge to continue in the fullness of life.

Your years in my care have blessed me as I have watched the unfolding of your life. It is with pride and tenderness that I now release that life to follow its own promise. I love you. I believe in you. I wish only the best for you.

THE TWENTY-FIFTH DAY

My child, you leave my home but not my heart.

What are the things I have always longed to do if only I had more time?

What interests were interrupted as I put the needs of my family first?

What calls my attention at this time of transition and discovery?

Your years in my care have blessed me as I have watched the unfolding of your life. It is with pride and tenderness that I now

release that life to follow its own promise. I love you. I believe in you. I wish only the best for you.

THE TWENTY-SIXTH DAY

My child, you leave my home but not my heart.

It is time now to say, in my own words, what is deepest in my heart:

....

Your years in my care have blessed me as I have watched the unfolding of your life. It is with pride and tenderness that I now release that life to follow its own promise. I love you. I believe in you. I wish only the best for you.

THE TWENTY-SEVENTH DAY

My child, you leave my home but not my heart.

Being a parent is an honor. It has brought me such wealth. In what ways can I share this treasure?
I will remember that the world is changed by people serving each other with devotion and gratitude in the name of the One.

Your years in my care have blessed me as I have watched the unfolding of your life. It is with pride and tenderness that I now release that life to follow its own promise. I love you. I believe in you. I wish only the best for you.

THE TWENTY-EIGHTH DAY

My child, you leave my home but not my heart.

You take with you the seeds of the tradition and heritage of our family.
Carry them well.
This is a time of sadness and a time of sweetness, and I acknowledge what I expect you, too, will come to understand in time: that throughout life, the sadness and the sweetness lie side by side.

Your years in my care have blessed me with the unfolding of your life. It is with pride and tenderness that I now release that life to follow its own promise. I love you. I believe in you. I wish only the best for you.

Challenge

THERE IS A story that challenge and fear are close friends. Challenge climbs mountains while fear explores caves. Their relationship is a mystery to those around them because it seems they have little in common. The great secret is that they remind each other of themselves when they were young.

Challenge wears many faces and just as many hats, from a court date to a job interview to a serious illness that eludes cure. It is natural to be afraid of a call to the unknown. It is probably even healthy. What is not healthy is to let fear turn to paralysis.

When challenge comes to visit it is easy to pretend no one is home, but to hide from challenge is to deny the opportunities it brings along. One opportunity is the chance to clarify our aims. The way we think can influence the world we make. Giving ourselves conflicting information about an important goal (and most goals *are* challenges) can bring confusion and inertia.

Challenge is a dragon with a gift in its mouth. Tame the dragon and the gift is yours. Notice I did not say "kill" the dragon. To kill the dragon implies stumbling through our challenges using any available force.

This week of vigils presents a chance to consider both how we negotiate the process, as well as the hoped-for results. If we can adopt a spirit of elegance and command, then, regardless of the outcome, we will have strengthened our dignity and honed our skill for understanding challenge as invitation to growth.

A challenge is a wish destiny makes for me to risk, to trust, and to grow.

Challenge can overwhelm, especially if it includes the possibility of far-reaching change, but change is the means by which we grow.
It is helpful for me to break big challenges into smaller ones and to take them a step at a time.
This gradual approach can lessen frustrations and allow for better management of my physical and emotional strengths.

Challenge will always be part of living. True victory lies in welcoming it as teacher, mentor, and guide to the greater in myself.

THE SECOND DAY

A challenge is a wish destiny makes for me to risk, to trust, and to grow.

I need to ask myself what my choices are. Sometimes we forget to explore other avenues if the present one seems limited. Many people credit their success to an offbeat idea that appeared when it seemed that all was lost. In remembering to watch closely for overlooked options, I open myself to the wisdom and direction of the True Source.

Challenge will always be part of living. True victory lies in welcoming it as teacher, mentor, and guide to the greater in myself.

THE THIRD DAY

A challenge is a wish destiny makes for me to risk, to trust, and to grow.

Successful navigation through challenge requires careful consideration.
I need to determine which risks I am willing to take and which carry unacceptable degrees of potential danger and loss.
Intelligent risk in the face of uncertainty is a responsibility I need to assume with vigilant care.

Challenge will always be part of living. True victory lies in welcoming it as teacher, mentor, and guide to the greater in myself.

THE FOURTH DAY

A challenge is a wish destiny makes for me to risk, to trust, and to grow.

Timing plays an important part in opportunity.
Knowing when to act quickly and when to hesitate requires observation and intuition.
As I become aware of the pace and rhythm of this challenge, I am able to move with greater confidence.

Challenge will always be part of living. True victory lies in welcoming it as teacher, mentor, and guide to the greater in myself.

THE FIFTH DAY

A challenge is a wish destiny makes for me to risk, to trust, and to grow.

Let me become clear about how my mind works and how I reach decisions.
Whether it be through prayer, solitude, or quiet conversation with myself, I will look to develop my concentration and attention.

I will remember that attention is the first step toward resolution.

Challenge will always be part of living. True victory lies in welcoming it as teacher, mentor, and guide to the greater in myself.

THE SIXTH DAY

A challenge is a wish destiny makes for me to risk, to trust, and to grow.

It is time now for me to say, in my own words, what is deepest in my heart:

···

Challenge will always be part of living. True victory lies in welcoming it as teacher, mentor, and guide to the greater in myself.

THE SEVENTH DAY

A challenge is a wish destiny makes for me to risk, to trust, and to grow.

Sometimes it can be many years before we understand the outcome of our challenges, and it is reassuring to know that I have done my best.

To use every resource I have without undue attachment to the results is to open to freedom, trust, and creativity of spirit. It is to say, "Thy will be done."

Challenge will always be part of living. True victory lies in welcoming it as teacher, mentor, and guide to the greater in myself.

Regret

NOTHING INSTRUCTS QUITE like regret, but it does not have to be a harsh teacher if we can acknowledge our humanness and find it in our hearts to forgive ourselves. Forgiving others is not always easy, but forgiving ourselves can be even more complicated. Without this forgiveness, however, we withhold the permission necessary for a second chance.

The month before my mother died, she moved from her apartment, where she lived with reasonable independence, to a facility where she could be cared for in the face of her diminishing physical abilities. En route to sign the necessary papers I ached to bring her home with me, but thoughts about my job, my young son, and space restrictions got in the way of my heart. I did not realize that a few weeks later our time together would come to an end. I remember the exact stoplight where this inner struggle caused such pain, and it can still hurt to see that my priorities were so misplaced.

A year later I was assisting on a tour to study culture and

customs in Indonesia when an older traveler became ill. While the group made day tours, she remained in her room growing weaker and more unable to tend to her basic needs. She was determined "to ride this thing out" on her own and refused offers of assistance and medical help. Finally, one evening, I simply walked in and began to bathe and care for her. "This is not part of your job," she said. "You don't have to do this."

But I did. I told her that I had been unable to assist someone very dear at a time when it was needed and I wasn't going to make that mistake again. Something in me healed. Second chances come in many forms.

I am not suggesting that this experience absolved me of all regret about my mother, but it showed me that I had gained a measure of understanding. It dawned on me that the real second chance was the one to forgive myself.

When you turn your quiet attention to these vigils, consider adding your forgiveness as well. Forgiveness can bring the lessons that need to be learned within easier reach, and these lessons can help grow the clarity and wisdom needed to make decisions that carry fewer regrets.

THE FIRST DAY

Feelings of regret drift through me with their mood of reflection and remorse.

To feel regret is to know that I care about the way I express myself and the choices I make.

It is to admit that I can take responsibility for my mistakes.

Maybe I did the best I could, under the circumstances, but perhaps I did not.

Knowing the difference can bring insight and instruction.

May this regret be released into forgiveness, compassion, and grace.

THE SECOND DAY

Feelings of regret drift through me with their mood of reflection and remorse.

In acknowledging that I would handle things differently if I had another chance, I invite a deeper unfolding of my heart.

I know that I am a child of the Divine, but I am rooted in a very human life.
My progress through its challenges requires patience and the resolve to try again.

May this regret be released into forgiveness, compassion, and grace.

THE THIRD DAY

Feelings of regret drift through me with their mood of reflection and remorse.

Guilt and regret are often intertwined like lovers, but guilt has nothing to do with love and little to do with growing.
Separating the guilt from the regret allows me to admit my mistake and to take a fresh look at the situation.

May this regret be released into forgiveness, compassion, and grace.

THE FOURTH DAY

Feelings of regret drift through me with their mood of reflection and remorse.

Do I owe someone an apology? Do I owe myself an apology? Saying "I'm sorry" can release guilt and temper regret.

It can lift the hurt of my mistakes and allow me to walk without blame.

May this regret be released into forgiveness, compassion, and grace.

THE FIFTH DAY

Feelings of regret drift through me with their mood of reflection and remorse.

Regret can be a teacher, but it should not be a steadfast companion.
Being stuck in remorse causes undue pain and unnecessary drama.
As I value and come to terms with its lessons, I gradually relinquish my regret.

May this regret be released into forgiveness, compassion, and grace.

THE SIXTH DAY

Feelings of regret drift through me with their mood of reflection and remorse.

It is time now to say, in my own words, what is deepest in my heart:

May this regret be released into forgiveness, compassion, and grace.

THE SEVENTH DAY

Feelings of regret drift through me with their mood of reflection and remorse.

Perhaps my sense of self is a little unsteady now and I need to remember that my life is a work in progress.
Some days are graced with accomplishment and others with regret.
Yesterday's regrets can be the foundation of tomorrow's achievements if they are held with attention and balance in my heart.

May this regret be released into forgiveness, compassion, and grace.

forgiveness

THE WORD "FORGIVENESS" has such a soft and pleasing sound, but in practice it requires the determination to look always for the best in ourselves and others. Holding a grudge affects the way we consider everything around us. Think for a moment of the tense posture and brittle attitude that accompanies resentment. Forgiveness is the way to dissolve these bitter feelings and purify our hearts.

Sometimes there are people or activities we simply do not wish to invite into our lives. Experience has shown that their influence is disruptive and confusing. However, we can still wish them well while choosing not to become involved.

To forgive is to "give something instead" and so we can offer hopeful thoughts instead of harsh ones. This can be a tremendous release for the other person and for ourselves. Continuing to hold judgments and limited ideas for months and years cuts us off from one another. We become remote and disconnected. We remain wary and skeptical and are always on guard for transgressions. In freezing our pardon, we trap our aliveness.

Forgiveness and compassion hold hands like sisters and call forth a strength that relies one on the other. Our actions and behavior are influenced by our security or lack of it, our frustrations, and usually our compulsions. We readily forgive a child, but we forget that growing up is a lifelong process. To understand that we each do the best we can with the maturity we have enables us to allow each other our inevitable "mistakes" and to practice the art of true forgiveness.

THE FIRST DAY

Remove my reluctance, release my blame, and open my heart to forgiveness.

Show me how to surrender my hurt, anger, and judgment. As I live my belief in forgiveness, I acknowledge its power to cut through resentment and blame.

As I forgive, I open the way for others to join me in forgiveness, with the hope that together we may draw closer to the One Heart.

THE SECOND DAY

Remove my reluctance, release my blame, and open my heart to forgiveness.

I may have just reason to be angry with this person, with this situation, and with myself.

But if I look at my anger truthfully, I can invite it to move aside so that I may be able to forgive.

As I forgive, I open the way for others to join me in forgiveness, with the hope that together we may draw closer to the One Heart.

THE THIRD DAY

Remove my reluctance, release my blame, and open my heart to forgiveness.

The pain of injustice upsets me and makes me feel insecure. Hurts from my own mistakes and those of others can linger and corrode my heart.
In offering to exchange this pain for pardon I restore my self-esteem and participate in the living grace of the Divine.

As I forgive, I open the way for others to join me in forgiveness, with the hope that together we may draw closer to the One Heart.

THE FOURTH DAY

Remove my reluctance, release my blame, and open my heart to forgiveness.

How much of this affront has to do with parts of me that I keep hidden, sometimes even from myself?

My desire to hold on to resentment reveals something that needs reevaluation and change. I must recognize how much of this injury is my own responsibility.

As I forgive, I open the way for others to join me in forgiveness, with the hope that together we may draw closer to the One Heart.

THE FIFTH DAY

Remove my reluctance, release my blame, and open my heart to forgiveness.

There is no need to condone inappropriate or hurtful behavior.

I am forgiving the person not the act.

As I surrender my judgment of another, I liberate the energy and emotional resources to lift this invisible weight and affirm life renewed.

As I forgive, I open the way for others to join me in forgiveness, with the hope that together we may draw closer to the One Heart.

THE SIXTH DAY

Remove my reluctance, release my blame, and open my heart to forgiveness.

It is time now to say, in my own words, what is deepest in my heart:

....

As I forgive, I open the way for others to join me in forgiveness, with the hope that together we may draw closer to the One Heart.

THE SEVENTH DAY

Remove my reluctance, release my blame, and open my heart to forgiveness.

If forgiveness is the destination, compassion is the road home. The heart responds to compassion like an appeal from an old friend in the night, with reassurance and understanding.
I call on my soul's indwelling compassion to practice the golden fundamental of my faith, to bear no ill will, and to leave judgment in the hands of the Force that powers all life.

As I forgive, I open the way for others to join me in forgiveness, with the hope that together we may draw closer to the One Heart.

Giving Thanks

GRATITUDE IS THE language of the angels. They whisper it among themselves and sing of it in heavenly choirs. They give thanks for blessings and also for difficulties, knowing that both bring opportunities to draw nearer to the One.

Too often we fail to savor our thankfulness. We tend to say, "Okay. Great!" "Thanks a lot," and we are off to the next challenge, the next hoped-for reward. We miss the chance to enjoy the feeling of being wrapped in the warmth and grace of a prayerful thank-you.

Thanksgiving gives determination the reward it deserves. It is said that the minute we become determined about something, a thousand visible and invisible helpmates are drawn to lend their energy and power. I don't know if it is really a thousand, but usually our dreams come true with the help of others. Offering thanks gives us the chance to extend our gratitude to a larger circle and to acknowledge the True Source of all blessings.

My mother used to tell me, "It's not finished till it's thanked for." Thanksgiving completes a circle that usually begins in prayer, hope, and uncertainty. These vigils offer a way to complete and deepen your gratitude and to strengthen your natural connection to life's abundance.

THE FIRST DAY

My hopes are rewarded, my prayers answered, and my life affirmed.

In giving thanks I acknowledge and welcome this happiness. I allow it to become part of me, and I enjoy the gladness it brings.

With reverence and appreciation, my heart whispers, "Alleluia."

THE SECOND DAY

My hopes are rewarded, my prayers answered, and my life affirmed.

It is important to remember that prayers are always answered, though sometimes not in the ways we expect nor at the times we might choose.
But *this* is a time when I can understand the answer and rejoice in its gift of resolution.

The circle is completed as I offer my thanks back to the One from whom all blessings flow.

With reverence and appreciation, my heart whispers, "Alleluia."

THE THIRD DAY

My hopes are rewarded, my prayers answered, and my life affirmed.

The ceremonial world is a place where I can integrate the things that happen to me and honor my passages. Is this the time for a personal ceremony to express my joy?
In what ways can I celebrate this happiness that will allow me to bring it more fully into my awareness?

With reverence and appreciation, my heart whispers, "Alleluia."

THE FOURTH DAY

My hopes are rewarded, my prayers answered, and my life affirmed.

One way to say thank you is to pass the blessings onto others. This is gratitude in action.
Sometimes the others have nothing to do with the current

miracle. The fact that they are in need of something that I can give is enough.

The One Life wears many disguises.

With reverence and appreciation, my heart whispers, "Alleluia."

THE FIFTH DAY

My hopes are rewarded, my prayers answered, and my life affirmed.

To be humble in the face of reward is to remember our connection to spirit and to all things.
I will strive to appreciate this richness with humility.
I will remember that modesty and graciousness are qualities that are always appropriate.

With reverence and appreciation, my heart whispers, "Alleluia."

THE SIXTH DAY

My hopes are rewarded, my prayers answered, and my life affirmed.

It is time now to say, in my own words, what is deepest in my heart:

With reverence and appreciation, my heart whispers, "Alleluia."

THE SEVENTH DAY

My hopes are rewarded, my prayers answered, and my life affirmed.

Spend some, save some, and share some: This counsel applies
to windfalls of the heart as well as of the purse.
How can I share this blessing in a way that will multiply its
riches?
Who believed in me when my own belief was uncertain?
Whose love has been constant even when I was distant and
preoccupied?
Who helped me to see through doubt to possibility?
Who reminded me to be patient and to expect the best?
Let me share my happiness with others—now, and always.

With reverence and appreciation, my heart whispers, "Alleluia."

Personal Violation

IT IS PAINFUL to acknowledge that violation is often an inescapable part of our lives, whether it is a breach of trust by someone close or a reckless assault by a stranger. It can take the form of emotional or sexual abuse, a robbery in our home, or an attack on the street, but whatever the circumstances, we may feel helpless and extremely vulnerable. The anguish and isolation from other people sometimes seem insufferable because such an act is a searing invasion of privacy. Our sense of control shatters and we are left to look for ways to heal the unspeakable.

Indeed, until quite recently, unspeakable is exactly what these kinds of experiences have been, but now attitudes are changing and people are learning that there is strength and comfort in sharing. In the past, sexual offenders, for instance, could hide behind the distorted protection of shame and silence, but if we can learn to speak of what has happened, not only do we spare ourselves the damage of repressed feelings and emotions, but we help prevent this tragedy from happening to others.

There were incidents in my childhood that I have spent years trying to forget. I have struggled to speak truthfully about them and to understand that we live in a world where each of us has the capacity for kindness and cruelty.

Finally, we must ask ourselves, "How can I use this injustice to strengthen my life?" This is a tough question. These vigils are a way of beginning this inquiry and are a first step on the difficult journey from victim to survivor.

THE FIRST DAY

I shudder in dismay as the shadow of violation moves across my life.

The chilling reality of what has happened leaves shock and disbelief in its wake.
My trust is shattered and I feel vulnerable and fragile.

My fear, anger, and tears bear witness to my healing and recovery.

THE SECOND DAY

I shudder in dismay as the shadow of violation moves across my life.

I try to push away the memories and pictures in my mind, but they recur with unforgiving frequency.
Although these reminders are painful, the events themselves are in the past.
At this moment I am safe, and I will look for ways to reinforce this safety.

My fear, anger, and tears bear witness to my healing and recovery.

THE THIRD DAY

I shudder in dismay as the shadow of violation moves across my life.

At times I feel shamed, although there is nothing to be ashamed of.
At times I feel negligent, although I know I am not at fault.
I try to make sense of something that seems senseless.

My fear, anger, and tears bear witness to my healing and recovery.

THE FOURTH DAY

I shudder in dismay as the shadow of violation moves across my life.

I cannot help wondering, "Why me?"
In an effort to regain my power, I strive to acknowledge the unfortunate reality that our world includes those whose twisted need for control results in the domination and wounding of others.
There is no correct way to respond to what has happened.
Whatever my response, it was the right one.

My fear, anger, and tears bear witness to my healing and recovery.

THE FIFTH DAY

I shudder in dismay as the shadow of violation moves across my life.

Anger and indignation begin to surface.
Perhaps the urgency of these feelings can be the catalyst I need
to speak with clarity and dignity about what took place.
The history of personal violation is cloaked in silence and
secrecy. To refuse to participate in the silence is to break a link
in the ugly chain of this kind of abuse.

My fear, anger, and tears bear witness to my healing and recovery.

THE SIXTH DAY

I shudder in dismay as the shadow of violation moves across my life.

It is time now for me to say, in my own words, what is deepest
in my heart:

....

My fear, anger, and tears bear witness to my healing and recovery.

THE SEVENTH DAY

I shudder in dismay as the shadow of violation moves across my life.

I need to remember that others have experienced this trauma
and have formed support systems and safety nets.
This passage is not one I have to make on my own.
As I discover and participate in the resources that are available
to me, I step into a powerful community of shared strength,
understanding, and help.

My fear, anger, and tears bear witness to my healing and recovery.

Acknowledgments

Grateful acknowledgment is made to the following people for the use of their words:

1. Susan Thaler, in the story "Vinnie's Angel" copyright © 1990 by Susan Thaler
2. Elizabeth Cogburn
3. Michael L. Lindvall

This book could not have been written without the encouragement of my family, the guidance of Evelyn Payne and Clarissa, the enthusiasm of Patti Breitman, the elegant hand of Toinette Lippe, and the life counsel of Elizabeth Cogburn.

ABOUT THE AUTHOR

NOELA N. EVANS lives in Northport, New York, in an old house overlooking the harbor, with her husband, son, and two cats, and her son's iguana.

OTHER BELL TOWER BOOKS

The pure sound of the bell summons us into the present moment.
The timeless ring of truth
is expressed in many different voices,
each one magnifying and illuminating the sacred.
The clarity of its song resonates within us
and calls us away from
those things which often distract us—
that which was, that which might be—
to That Which Is.

Being Home: *A Book of Meditations*
by Gunilla Norris
An exquisite modern book of hours, a celebration
of mindfulness in everyday activities.
Hardcover 0-517-58159-0 1991

Nourishing Wisdom: *A Mind/Body Approach*
to Nutrition and Well-Being
by Marc David
A practical way out of dietary confusion, a book that
advocates awareness in eating and reveals how our attitude
to food reflects our attitude to life.
Softcover 0-517-88129-2 1994

Sanctuaries: The Northeast
A Guide to Lodgings in Monasteries, Abbeys, and Retreats of
the United States
by Jack and Marcia Kelly
The first in a series of regional guides for those in search of
renewal and a little peace.
Softcover 0-517-57727-5 1991

Grace Unfolding
Psychotherapy in the Spirit of the Tao-te ching
by Greg Johanson and Ron Kurtz
The interaction of client and therapist illuminated through
the gentle power and wisdom of Lao Tzu's ancient Chinese classic.
Softcover 0-517-88130-6 1994

Self-Reliance: The Wisdom of Ralph Waldo Emerson as
Inspiration for Daily Living
Selected and with an introduction by Richard Whelan
A distillation of Emerson's essential spiritual writings for
contemporary readers.
Softcover 0-517-58512-X 1991

Compassion in Action: Setting Out on the Path of Service
by Ram Dass and Mirabai Bush
Heartfelt encouragement and advice for those ready to
commit time and energy to relieving suffering in the world.
Softcover 0-517-57635-X 1992

Letters from a Wild State
Rediscovering Our True Relationship to Nature
by James G. Cowan
A luminous interpretation of Aboriginal spiritual experience
applied to the leading issue of our time: the care of the earth.
Hardcover 0-517-58770-X 1992

Silence, Simplicity, and Solitude
A Guide for Spiritual Retreat
by David A. Cooper
This classic guide to meditation and other traditional
spiritual practice is required reading for anyone
contemplating a retreat.
Softcover 0-517-88186-1 1994

The Heart of Stillness
The Elements of Spiritual Practice
by David A. Cooper
A primer of spiritual discipline, a comprehensive guidebook
to the basic principles of inner work—a companion volume
to Silence, Simplicity, and Solitude.
Hardcover 0-517-58621-5 1992
Softcover 0-517-88187-x 1994

One Hundred Graces
Selected by Marcia and Jack Kelly
With calligraphy by Christopher Gausby
A collection of mealtime graces from many traditions,

beautifully inscribed in calligraphy reminiscent of the
manuscripts of medieval Europe.
Hardcover 0-517-58567-7 1992
Softcover 0-517-88230-2 1995

Sanctuaries: The West Coast and Southwest
A Guide to Lodgings in Monasteries, Abbeys, and Retreats
of the United States
by Marcia and Jack Kelly
The second volume of what The New York Times called
"the Michelin Guide of the retreat set."
Softcover 0-517-88007-5 1993

Becoming Bread
Meditations on Loving and Transformation
by Gunilla Norris
A book linking the food of the spirit—love—with the food
of the body—bread. More meditations by the author of
Being Home.
Hardcover 0-517-59168-5 1993

Messengers of the Gods
Tribal Elders Reveal the Ancient Wisdom of the Earth
by James G. Cowan
A lyrical and visionary attempt to understand the
metaphysical landscape of Northern Australia and the
islands just beyond it.
By the author of Letters from a Wild State.
Softcover 0-517-88078-4 1993

Pilgrimage to Dzhvari
A Woman's Journey of Spiritual Awakening
by Valeria Alfeyeva
A powerful and eloquent account of a contemporary Russian woman's
discovery of her Christian heritage.
A modern Way of a Pilgrim.
Hardcover 0-517-59194-4 1993

The Journal of Hildegard of Bingen
by Barbara Lachman
A liturgical year in the life of the twelfth-century German mystic, abbess,
composer, and healer. This fictional diary is the one she never had the time
to write herself.
Hardcover 0-517-59169-3 1993

Sharing Silence
Meditation Practice and Mindful Living
by Gunilla Norris
A simple practical manual of the essential conditions for meditation and
for life itself. By the author of Being Home *and* Becoming Bread.
Hardcover 0-517-59506-0 1993

Entering the Sacred Mountain
A Mystical Odyssey
by David A. Cooper
An inspiring chronicle of one man's search for truth,
exploring the esoteric practices of Judaism, Buddhism, and Islam.
Hardcover 0-517-59653-9 1994

The Alchemy of Illness
by Kat Duff
A luminous inquiry into the function and purpose of illness.
Softcover 0-517-88097-0 1994

A Walk Between Heaven and Earth
A Personal Journal on Writing and the Creative Process
by Burghild Nina Holzer
How keeping a journal focuses and expands our awareness of ourselves
and everything that touches our lives.
Softcover 0-517-88096-2 1994

Journeying in Place
Reflections from a Country Garden
by Gunilla Norris
Another classic book of meditations,
illuminating the sacredness of daily experience.
Hardcover 0-517-59762-4 1994

Chant
The Origins, Form, Practice, and Healing Power of Gregorian Chant
by Katharine Le Mée
A book that explains the extraordinary effects
of this ancient liturgical singing.
Hardcover 0-517-70037-9 1994

Bell Tower books are for sale at your local bookstore, or you may call
1-800-793-BOOK and order with a credit card.